Buddhist Existentialism

From Anxiety to Authenticity and Freedom

MEANING-VALUE: 97
Existential Assumptions: 58f

Buddhist Existentialism

from anxiety to authenticity and freedom

The Rose Is Without Why

Dr Robert Miller

SHOGAM
PUBLICATIONS

Shogam Publications
Carlton North, Victoria, 3054
www.shogam.org

National Library of Australia
Cataloguing-in-Publication data:
Miller, Robert, 1952– .
Buddhist existentialism: from anxiety to authenticity and
freedom / Robert Miller.
ISBN 978-0-9805022-0-6 (pbk.)
Includes Index.
Bibliography.
1 Buddhism. 2 Existentialism. 3 Buddhism—Philosophy
294.307

Cover design by Mila Nikko ©IDEE
Cover photography by Catherine Acin

The rose is without why;
It blooms because it blooms;
It cares not for itself, asks not if it's seen.

— Angelus Silesius
The Cherubinic Wanderer, I: 289.

CONTENTS

INVITATION TO THE READER

Okay, there are rather a lot of words here. After all, I am a philosopher. However, I have found in the end that the best approach to life is to frequently practice a kind of close sympathetic nonjudgmental attention to things—a kind of wordless aesthetic attention to what is that tends to heighten a sense of stillness and beauty. Then, when it comes to adopting a reasoned philosophy to surround and support this practice, a way of thinking about the nature of life and reality, why not try positing a maximally positive and beautiful vision—non-dogmatically, of course—until or unless someone can prove the worse is true? Which they can never do: see inside for reasons why.

This double game of philosophical reasoning and aesthetic contemplation (of reflection and de-reflection) seems to aid toward the re-enchantment and self-enjoyment of life. Things get less heavy: one feels lighter. Of course, the game only applies if one is interested in en-lightening life in some such way. Whether you want to or not is up to you. Each to his own!

But it's a trip to consider…

1

VOIDANCE AND EXISTENTCE ITSELF

Existence itself is not hung up.
– Allen Ginsberg

WE WILL BEGIN by focusing on the meaning of the doctrine of *shunyata* as developed in Nagarjuna's (243–300 AD) *Madhyamaka* (Middle Way) philosophy and consider its potential benefits for our wellbeing, enlightenment and re-enchantment. T. R. V. Murti maintains that the Madhyamaka philosophy, with its key concept of shunyata (usually translated as voidance, emptiness, nothingness, openness) is the central philosophy of Buddhism.[1] Most scholars regard Nagarjuna as the most important Buddhist philosopher and a figure in the history of Buddhism second only in importance to Gautama Buddha (563–483 BC) himself. So we are dealing here with fundamental Buddhism.

SHUNYATA

Some people will say there is something even *more* fundamental in Buddhism, and that is the philosophy of the *Four Noble Truths* and the *Eightfold Noble Path*. However, it can be argued that the idea of shunyata (emptiness, voidance) follows logically from the Four Noble Truths and so is crucial to the Eightfold Path. This can be explained as follows. The First Noble Truth tells us that all ordinary life in the world is full of *duhkha* (usually translated as dis-ease, disquiet, troubles, conflict or suffering). The Second Noble Truth tells us that the cause is *tanha*, which might best be translated as 'grasping'—an unwise grasping and clinging that has both an intellectual (or cognitive) and a passionate (or affective) component.

The affective component refers to our emotional and feeling states, our states of emotional grasping, desiring and wanting and being *attached* to those wants. An emotional dependency, a clinging and craving, is implied. We normally have an attachment or addiction to possessing and holding securely our various objects of desire in the vain hope of making them stable, permanent and thereby reliable as sources of happiness. We cleave to the objects of desire with a kind of desperation, mistakenly believing we really need them or that we absolutely *must have* them if we are to be happy and at peace in life.

The cognitive component refers to our intellectual attempts to grasp at the nature of reality in this or that theory or belief-system and so capture and possess reality securely in concepts. One wants to have 'the true view' (as we like to think) or 'the true concept' of reality, make the true judgement and so possess and master the truth of life, holding fast to *that* object as permanent, fixed and reliable for our happiness and peace of mind.

However, the basic characteristic of human life is that neither the objects of desire nor the objects of thought actually *are* reliable in the way we would like to think they are. Rather, they are all vulnerable to the ongoing flux of life: to impermanence, to change, to destruction, to doubt and uncertainty, to general defeat and decay. In short, they are not permanently or reliably grounded or fixed. They are not well-founded, as we might say. They are insecure. No wonder then we are so insecure! Our deep disquiet (*duhkha*) in life arises because we try to rely for peace of mind and happiness on these inherently unreliable and insecure objects that can't really be relied on for peace and happiness and that tend to divert and distract us from what *can* be relied on for peace or happiness (we will come to that shortly).

Because we try to grasp at everything to fixate it—passionately and intellectually, affectively and cognitively—we find we are forever being frustrated by the fleeting movement of life itself, the groundless flux, the changes everything goes through. We are frustrated and dissatisfied, made restless or discontent, because life and reality does not yield itself to our egocentric grasping ways, our quest for permanence in an impermanent world. Our life in this world will just not stay fixed! (Strictly speaking, not even from one minute to the next). This kind of fretful frustration with the natural movement of life is again duhkha. And of course ordinary life is full of it.

We really need to get it into our head that everything flows and changes and learn how to become in harmony with this flow and change—or let's say, learn how to *become* in harmony with *becoming*. ✓

The Madhyamaka philosophy is a teaching that shows us that our belief-systems and the intellectual judgements we make about the nature of self and reality, or about what ultimately really *is*, are all im- ✓ permanent and changeable over time because they are all inherently questionable, dubious, non-provable, unfixable, insecure—or in a word: *empty* (null and void). This emptiness or voidance of all theoretical and conceptual constructions or simulations of reality is summed up in the notion of shunyata. Everything about the nature of reality mediated by language and thought and taken to be a truth is *shunyata*—voidable, voided.

The aim of this philosophy is not to leave us utterly bereft of all thought or views, or lacking in concepts or beliefs about reality, for then we would not be able to function! Rather, the aim is to empower ✓ and enable us, by way of our reasoned inquiry and self-developed critical understanding, to be non-addicted or non-attached in relation to our language, thoughts, views, concepts and beliefs about the nature of reality. In other words, just as it may be said to be en-lightened (or wise) to *have* desires if the desires *do not have us*, as it were, so we may *have* language, thoughts, views, concepts and beliefs, *if* they *do not*

philosophy = a way of living

have us. That is, if they do not so possess and obsess us that we are emotionally attached or addicted to them and can't shrug them off or drop them. We won't be such emotionally troubled *addicts* as long as we are able to critically 'see through' and readily 'let go' of our habitual thoughts and desires in a special act of meditation (that we will get to in due course).

This idea fits neatly with the Noble Truths. For the Third Noble Truth is that the Buddha has found a cure for our suffering and that this cure is non-attachment to the objects of thought and desire. No wonder Buddhism is often referred to as 'the way of non-attachment'. The Madhyamaka applies this non-attachment in a very radical manner to language, human views, belief-systems about the nature of reality, thought-forms and judgements.

The Madhyamaka philosophy of Nagarjuna is a classic example of what is called a *critical dialectic*. It reflects critically, systematically and radically on virtually every kind of theory or view that human beings have ever taken of the nature of reality. It probes and undermines all such theories by raising various arguments and pertinent questions against them. It shows no inquiring rational person can take any theory of reality to be true, dogmatically fixed or self-certain. For our various belief-systems are, for example, overtly or subtly *self-contradictory* (internally incoherent) in some way, or they require *leaps of logic* beyond what can be properly or rigorously established or proved. In short, a little critical reflection shows our belief-systems are full of holes. This is where the light gets in.

In what follows, I will refrain from going into the actual content of Nagarjuna's own critical dialectic and text and the specific arguments he uses to undermine all views. There are two reasons why I am refraining from this here. First, because the arguments as they actually occur in the text are quite difficult to summarise and explicate in our modern setting. They are expressed in rather obscure ways for the Westerner and layperson to follow. For many of the views criticised were views popular in Nagarjuna's own time and place, but they are not so familiar or relevant to most of us today. Secondly, I think much the same thing—*the radical undermining of addiction to language and belief*—can be presented in an easier way for Westerners and laypeople to follow. For we have in our own philosophical tradition, comparable arguments that arrive at a similar result. It will be easier for us to look to those more familiar philosophical arguments to arrive at 'detachment from views,' rather than at Nagarjuna's own specific and complex arguments.

We will look at those more familiar Western arguments in the next chapter, so I will reserve the actual argumentation that can effectively undermine and dispose of the validity of views until then. For the time being, I will focus instead on the general intent lying behind critical dialectics and consider how and why this kind of approach is relevant to the cessation of duhkha. In other words, I will attempt to show in this chapter how and why such a critical dialectic can have a *soteriological* (a liberating, beneficial and enlightening) effect on our lives.

DUHKHA AND ITS CESSATION

SUFFERING

The central theme here is that we ourselves, with our 'unskilful' ways of fixated believing and desiring, create our own existential problems in everyday life. As American poet Allen Ginsberg (1926-1997) once said, 'existence itself is not hung-up,' by which he meant to imply we create our own existential hang-ups. We are, so to speak, our own worst enemies in this regard. We generate our troubles in our 'monkey-minds' and then project them on to life and reality, all the while thinking that they are inherent to reality—or inherent to what I will call *Existence Itself*. We claim that life and reality, the external factors in life, are to blame for our troubles, as if Existence Itself were hung-up or as if the hang-ups are somehow built-in and therefore unavoidable in human existence. Existence Itself, however, is void (*shunyata*) of hang-ups. This is the basic Buddhist idea. The hang-ups are only in our imaginary and dubious interpretations or conceptual constructions of life and reality, our fundamental reality-assumptions,

quote

superimposed by us onto life and reality. The troubles exist only in and by those constructs or assumptions; the language games we play with reality. But we can undermine them. Good!

x quote

One might put it that the 'gospel' (the 'evangel' or *good news*) in the Buddhist teaching is that, if we can undermine and let go of the dogmatism and fixity of our linguistic constructs and assumptions so we cease clinging to them, or cease grasping at life and reality through them, we can learn to dissolve our hang-ups, our troubles, our disquiet. We will then be, as it were, restored to the aesthetic quality (of feeling and mood) of Existence Itself, as it is 'originally,' in itself, as it is, devoid (*shunyata*) of such constructs and hang-ups.

Our hang-ups are duhkha. We are here talking about the means to the *cessation of duhkha*—and that is the Buddhist goal. That is the program. Let us see if we can get with it.

We can restore ourselves to the aesthetic quality of Existence Itself and let go of our hang-ups or so-called troubles in life, *if* we can deeply realise that our conceptual constructs of reality have no real or fundamental validity—or fixed 'self-existence', as the Madhyamikas also put it—that is, if we can realise that they are not basic or stable or necessary to reality but are only a kind of network of linguistic assumptions we superimpose on it. After all, people in different times and places project different assumptions. They are contingent, changeable and variable. To say that our human thoughts and beliefs are not inherent to reality, or that they are not 'the given truth' as such, is to say they are not absolute or essential. (This *anti-essentialism* is a point we will return to when we discuss *existentialism* in chapter three).

However, human beings tend to believe that their conceptual constructs and metaphysical worldviews are absolute, valid, true and essential. They too quickly assume and take it for granted that the belief-systems have some self-existence, some absolute right of existence and validity of their own, rather than just being something that exists only relative to ourselves as our own cultural language, mental projection, and questionable bias—a reflection of our own partial, fragmented, culturally, personally or linguistically *skewed* perspective on life and reality. Making this move, we fall into *delusion*, which here means taking our various biased beliefs and perspectives for the absolute. The Madhyamaka teaching and way of meditation aims to liberate and save us from precisely this delusion.

Our hang-ups are duhkha; our deep existential disquiet is created by living in delusion. Delusion is being attached to the imaginary metaphysical constructions we superimpose on Existence Itself as if they were true and absolute. If we could just drop our delusion, we could drop our duhkha. This dropping occurs in shunyata meditation, where we dissolve away our thought-centred disquiet and so bring ourselves in clarity and openness (shunyata) to a new kind of inner wellbeing. Peace gathers. However, it seems there is one supreme stumbling block to this, a major barrier that curtails our freedom to finding this kind of release.

It is as follows. Believing as we do that our conceptual constructions are both essential and given as true, and so have a kind of absolute self-existence of their own, we believe that we are *unable* to void them. We *think* they are true, therefore, we feel we are basically stuck with them; wedded to them whether we like it or not. From this kind of standpoint, it is simply impossible for us to see that they are variable, violable, voidable, that they can be cancelled, annulled and shown to be null and void—shunyata. Also, probably we don't realise that it might be a good thing to violate and void them, because we are so used to relying on them for our sense of self-identity, security and orientation to life.

The block to our self-liberation from self-torment is that we are stuck in the habit of *believing in* our so-called knowledge and truths. We trust them, so much so, we take our interpretation to be the real itself—ultimate, non-deceptive and non-delusional. We assume, with hardly a second thought, that we are not comprehensively deceived by our particular conditioning in this or that cultural neck of the woods. We ignore the possibility we are mistaken in holding so fast to our convictions about our self and our life, about others and about metaphysical reality. We cling to our beliefs and won't let go! Now that is grasping. That is attachment. That is holding on with a mind like a tight fist!

The aim of the Madhyamaka is to get us to release our grip. It provokes us to stop now and reflect critically and insightfully on all our various thought-constructions to show that they are not essential truths, that they do not have ultimate validity or absolute self-existence. They are not simply 'the given' with regard to reality. This can be done by showing that our belief-systems are all highly *questionable* as such, either because they are self-contradictory or inconsistent, or they involve us in unwarranted leaps of logic, or they are views that have no more grounds or arguments in their favour than directly *opposite* views.

Taking it a stage further, the dialectic reveals not only that no theory or view of the ultimate nature of reality is given as essential or true, but that no theory or view stands out as being more *probably* true than any other. Nothing we can say about the ultimate nature of reality is more *probably* correct than anything else we might say about it—even if we may happen to strongly feel or intuit it is—for we could be radically deceived and mistaken in even our strongest feelings and intuitions. After all, people from diverse cultures have had very different feelings and intuitions about the true nature of things. The strength of feeling or the assurance of intuition is quite simply *not* a proof of truth.

The critical logic of such reflections can bring us to a kind of profound *silence* about metaphysics, about reality. We may find we are struck dumb as it were; intelligently dumbfounded in the moment of critical awareness, surprised by doubt and suddenly opened to the absolute mystery of immediate existence here and now. Realising that all conceptual constructions, thoughts and words, are ultimately imaginary and speculative, we see that Existence Itself is void (*shunyata*) of these structures; they are not inherent to reality. Therefore, we gain some detachment from them, dissociate from them and put them in abeyance. Existence Itself is suddenly restored to its purity or original wonderment for us. And then, to borrow a famous phrase from Ludwig Wittgenstein (1889–1951), we might put it that, 'Whereof one cannot speak, thereof one must remain silent'.[2] Well, at least temporarily!

This critically induced silence—silence spontaneously born of sudden critical insight and understanding—is perhaps the most skilful or intelligent silence and mode of meditation. This meditation practice is not about endless chanting or navel gazing, it is about awakening our critical intelligence in any moment of life. It is about being able to let go of cultural language and all dubious mental mediations and constructions. It is about practising non-attachment. It is about being there in that clearing: all beliefs suspended in uncanny openness.

Because the so-called self or ego is also empty of any conceptual construction, the so-called self or ego is restored to the original purity of Existence Itself *without separation*—that is, in a non-dualistic way. In other words, the conceptual construction we superimpose on ourselves—the usual way we view ourselves, or think about ourselves as a separate, continuous, self-subsistent ego—has no real self-existence, is not absolute or essential or the given truth as such. It too is shunyata, *voided and voidable*, as is our view of the world itself as a separate entity. Non-dualism means: one is not attached to duality.

Seeing this, *seeing through* the image of oneself as a separate personal self-identity in time, or a separate being or entity, we are restored to non-separate or non-dual Existence Itself as devoid of ontological distinctions and divisions. There are no grounds, in other words, for believing in any real distinction or separation of the so-called self from the so-called not-self. For these conceptions of self and not-self, the idea of oneself as something essentially different from, and other than, the not-self—the 'other,' others, the rest of the world, the whole movement of life, fate and destiny, etcetera—are likewise *voided* concepts and beliefs.

When all such concepts are cancelled and annulled one is restored to the aesthetic quality of non-dual Existence Itself. Then, in

this meditation, there is *only* the aesthetic quality of non-dual Existence Itself at that point: one is assimilated to it. And since *Existence
Itself is not hung-up*, you yourself are not hung-up—for there is no
'you' separate from Existence Itself as the supposed creator or victim
of such hang-ups. Personal hang-ups are voided. Troubles are voided.
They are seen to be empty of real being or truth or validity. All your
troubles are shunyata. Seeing deeply into this, one is free of them:
non-attached. There is simply a non-dual here-and-now existence in
voidance, with no grounds for any sense of division or conflict with
what is or *is-ness* in general. After all, for all one knows at that point,
everything is one and perfect and exactly as it should be. One simply
has no grounds for a comment about it either way. There is the voidance of assumptions; the quietude of voidness.

EXISTENCE ITSELF

What is this Existence Itself, this Existence de-voided of conceptual
constructs? We cannot say that it is something discreet and static,
some sort of static being, immutable and eternal (as some philosophers say) or as something coming into being as a kind of momentary
flashing into existence from nothingness, complete and whole (as
some other philosophers say, notably many Buddhists). On the other
hand, we cannot say that it is the result of, or part of, some continuous causal process arising out of a presumed past and moving
into a presumed future (as some other philosophers say). We cannot
say it is made of matter only (as materialists say), or that it is made
up of matter and mind (as mind-body dualists say) or that it is made
up only of mind (as idealist philosophers say). We can't say any of this
because to think of Existence Itself in some such way would be to re-
conceptualise it again, to superimpose yet another dogmatic linguistic
construction upon it—meanwhile imagining that this construction is
something given as essential and true, or that it has self-existence or
that it is the absolute.

If we imagine reality being thus or so, being this or that, we

would no longer have Existence Itself but rather a conceptual imposition masquerading as a truth. Rather, in meditation, we remain in-
sightful and awake; intelligently silent and open to experiencing the
aesthetic quality of Existence Itself, in its original purity and mystery,
voided of assumptions. It is simple really, just suspend all your assumptions, at least temporarily. And when you think and speak
again—perhaps in the very next moment—realise that you are thinking and speaking voidable assumptions. That way, one doesn't fall
back into delusion, into attachment to assumptions.

One might follow Zen in referring to this kind of meditation as a
matter of restoring 'original mind' or the original purity of what
is—or the impenetrable mystery of nothingness, meaning: no-thing-
ness (since reality can be named as this or that 'thing'). There is
nowhere for thought to 'cling' in the voidance. Now, if there is nowhere for thought to cling, why then would one even need to 'wipe
the mirror mind clean,'[3] by actively trying to repress or silence
thoughts in meditation? If one clearly perceives the voidness, there is
no need for this wiping, because there is nowhere for thought-forms
(ideas, beliefs, etcetera) to cling: they come and go as voided. They
pass like fluffy clouds in the sky, like empty rainbow bubbles in the
mind. One can simply let them bubble up and dissolve again—much
ado about nothing. Actually, at this point, in this meditation, everything is much ado about nothing, and one can let go of it as such.
Naturally, peace gathers.

The upshot of the Madhyamaka is simple: strictly speaking, ultimately, we cannot say anything at all about Existence Itself. It is
unspeakable. We can only experience it or live it within this immediate realisation in any moment—that is, in a critically intelligent
stillness and an inward silence non-attached to language. We do this
by insight, seeing through imposed conceptualisations as and when
they happen to arise in the mind for whatever reason (as they tend to
do spontaneously, automatically, by conditioning and habit or by
karma, etcetera). In short, we cease grasping at reality intellectually or
cognitively. We cease trying to *capture the flow of life in a conceptual*

box—that is, we cease trying to fixate it in *logocentric* (word-centred) explanations. Rather, we 'let go and let be' by getting our selves and our beliefs, our intellectual clinging and graspingness, out of the way. We restore life and ourselves to Existence Itself by de-conceptualising it—an instantaneous auto-destruction of the construct. Pure de-reflection, as it were.

This practice, this meditation, requires and presupposes a genuine critical insight and deep understanding that is truly one's own. It cannot really be done properly any other way. That is, this kind of quietude in the mind cannot be *forced* by some mechanical method or technique or ritual. An *enforced* silence of the mind is artificial, not a real and natural silence of the mind. That is why the various forms of meditation that rely heavily on willpower, ritual, self-discipline, repeating a practice or mantra, chanting, etcetera—as dictated per-haps by some external authority (e.g., some master or guru) to supposedly quiet the mind—don't really succeed in genuinely quieting the mind. At best, even when these methods seem to work, they only induce a temporary and rather benumbed quiescence, one that is shaky indeed and that can easily be interrupted or destroyed by further delusions arising in the mind. An imposed quiet is just waiting to burst out anew in disquiet—like a quiet imposed on a class of unruly school kids. At best, it's a temporary palliative, not a cure. Only continuous insight provides the cure.

One is inclined, therefore, to agree with Jiddu Krishnamurti (1895–1986) when he says that any meditation that is not firmly based on 'the awakening of intelligence,' as he calls it (in his book of that title) is a rather feeble kind of meditation, or even a futile and mind-dulling meditation, or a merely obedient, repetitive or imitative kind of meditation—not the kind of meditation that might genuinely liberate us and that we have truly made our own through 'skilful understanding' in daily practice.

T. R. V. Murti seems to claim that the critical dialectic and void-ness is only applied in a preliminary way to eliminate conceptual knowledge in order to 'create room' for a new transcendental 'intellectual intuition' to arise. This would supposedly be some kind of unitive, intuitive, quasi-mystical way of experiencing and re-conceiving the ultimate reality—something like a mystical revelation perhaps, in which the absolute reality behind illusory appearances or the absolute Oneness of everything, is shown in a supposedly self-validating way.[4] Thus, now we have yet another conceptualisation of reality itself masquerading as an absolute truth. Everything is One!

Frederick Streng, in his book on Emptiness, argues that this Murtian move is disallowed by the critical dialectic itself.[5] The dialectic cannot be a mere means to a purer or higher intellectual intuition of the true reality, or a mystical revelation of truth, or knowledge of the absolute, because any such experience, if it engenders some new theory or proposition—for example, that reality *really is* One and this is the essential *truth* of reality—would itself be undermined straightaway by further dialectical inquiry and criticism. Logically that seems so. Therefore, rather than dogmatic absolutism or mysticism, the goal of the critical dialectic is the undermining and letting go of all imaginary conceptual and linguistic constructions of reality that the mind superimposes on Existence Itself, whether they are commonsensical and dualistic or unitive and mystical.

The key experience according to the Madhyamaka teaching is not something mystical and transcendental. It is more simply: the ordinary and everyday conceptualised experience of life, where we now have direct critical insight into the voidable nature of this conceptualised or linguistically interpreted reality, and consequently, do not become emotionally addicted to it, or any part of it, as if to something real, essential, self-existent, absolute, closed, final or ultimately valid. We void it. Nothing clings. There is letting go.[6]

We experience the conceptualised and divided reality just as it is for ordinary linguistic consciousness—and so as the Chinese saying goes, 'Everyday mind is the Tao'—but we also understand that this conceptualised and divided reality is only a provisional construction of the mind, not something to take as the true or absolute reality, as something ultimate or a matter of 'ultimate concern' that is a serious problem or source of serious problems. The key practice is just to void everything and see through our language game of reality. This restores us to the pure aesthetic quality of Existence Itself in original wonderment free from dualities and personal hang-ups—duhkha.

As we lose our deep-rooted addiction to the belief in ontological dualities, to all fixed ideas involving a persisting personal self and an external world of separate people and discreet objects (our usual dualistic metal map or simulation of the world, in other words) so we lose our deep-rooted addiction to our temporal objects of desire as well—hence our hang-ups too. Our troubles are not thereby 'solved' as such, but rather they are, along with ego and world, 'dissolved'—annulled in the nothingness, so to speak, in the void. There is no clinging and craving in that voidance: hence no conflict or troubles. We chill out completely. That would have to be the ultimate in cool. We can chill out completely in the void. Then we can come back into the world to rave or do our thing, but now in non-attachment to everything mediated by our cultural language, for we are never much removed from that tranquil and liberating shunyata-awareness.

Duhkha is a state of disease born of addiction. It is our everyday existential suffering and disquiet, our uneasy mental and emotional turmoil, our basic conflict with life. The suffering can take on many forms, of course, but the different forms have the same root. In general the suffering is generated by frustrated desire as such, which is in turn generated by grasping and clinging on to impermanent unreliable thoughts and things. We are troubled when our will is thwarted and when we experience this thwarting as bothersome to us, as a valid cause for suffering. This occurs when we cannot or do not get what we believe we want, or when we get what we believe we don't want or even in just being aware of the ongoing possibility of this happening; for that creates distress in the form of worry and self-concern.

Duhkha, therefore, is really about being in a state of personal conflict with present moments just as they are: as they happen or as they might happen. Underlying this, as the fundamental ground for this conflict and experience of frustration, is this or that assumption we make about life—about how life *should be*, about *what it should provide for us*, about what *ideals* we *ought to be attaining*, about what is *good or bad* in what is happening to us, about what we ourselves really are and what *we supposedly deserve*, about what others are and supposedly deserve, about what the real and ultimate causes are for our current experiences, about what *really* exists or does not exist, about what our life and death *really* is, about the *meaning* of it all and so on. Prejudices about such matters generate our frustration in life, as does our fixated belief that we have some true grounds for regarding life and reality, fate or circumstances, as separate from us and potentially bad or hostile. We assume that life and reality is *capable* of 'not going our way,' which assumes we are something separate from it. This assumption is dissolved in non-dual emptiness. When belief in division is voided and we detach from this belief, the sense of being in conflict with life and reality dissipates. Harmony arises of itself.

Above all, it is our *separative* way of thinking and believing that generates our addiction to our wants, to our likes and dislikes, and to our anxious and hostile attitude to reality. The dogmatic thinking and believing doesn't cause wants and desires in themselves, since they can be caused by an endless number of things, such as genetic factors, biological factors, chemical factors, or perhaps even karmic factors. But it is not our 'wants' in themselves that are responsible for our emotional troubles: it is our addictions to our wants. *As addicts*, we take our wants and their fulfilment to have a supreme or absolute or essential importance and value. Insofar as it is possible for a person to want something, yet not be addicted or attached to this want, the 'not getting what is wanted' or the awareness of this possibility, will not be a problem for that person. One can 'take it or leave it,' as we say.

However, we surely will be addicted, and troubles surely will follow, if we regard the attainment of the objects of desire as something essential to us. And we will consider them essential if they are stipulated as being essential as a corollary to the conceptual construction of reality we are in the habit of projecting. Therefore, as long as we have such a dogmatically fixed view of life and reality we will also have some dogmatically fixed and essential values, goals, ideals or wants: that is, objectives we believe must be attained if our sense of inner wellbeing or happiness is to be preserved or enhanced.

As long as we are addicts to our desires, to our likes and dislikes, we will be emotionally dependent on them for our happiness. We will be, in effect, *slaves* to them, surely not a *noble* condition (hence The Four Noble Truths to counter this). Our happiness will be vulnerable to the vicissitudes of fate or the failure of present moments to be in accordance with our desires. This failure, even awareness of the mere possibility of it, occasions our disease or duhkha. However, if addiction to desires turns on addiction to constructions of reality, then if we can let go of the latter, we can let go of the former; hence, this intellectual emancipation will have an emotional (soteriological) effect. Nagarjuna is showing that the way to enable it is via an education in critical dialectic—a *via negativa*, as it were—that reveals the voidance of views. Dissociating ourselves from views, especially separative or dualistic views, frees us from attachment to our desires as well and so brings about the weakening and cessation of duhkha—the goal of Buddhism.

According to Buddhism, we would do well to realise it is a commonplace folly to expect happiness to come from the pursuit of desires in the world and their fulfilment. For to think this way is to reinforce our dependency on them, and this, as the Buddha would say, is both ignoble and unprofitable. It is said to be 'ignoble' because, being such slaves to our desires, we will not be able to keep our moral precepts very well and maintain our personal moral integrity. We will tend to be fickle, untrustworthy, and unreliable, no matter how wonderful our moral ideals are, because our desires are fickle, untrustworthy and unreliable and we are driven and controlled by them. It is said to be 'unprofitable' because, being slaves to our desires, our happiness is at the mercy of all the so-called 'slings and arrows of outrageous fortune' on which the satisfaction of desires depends. That way madness lies!

For example, it is not that one should not, say, go to a party. But one should realise that happiness does not lie in the party as such: for it lies in yourself and how you approach each present moment, whether you are at a party or not. The important point, then, is not whether you go or don't go to a party, but to know how to approach each moment in a way that will promote wellbeing from within, regardless of the external circumstances. Only if we can realise this happiness from within, based on understanding and insight, will we be free masters of our desires. Only as free masters of our desires can we hope to be able to keep our moral precepts and remain inwardly happy at the same time, even despite all the vicissitudes of fate. So only this approach to life is both *noble* and *profitable*. It can only be achieved, according to the Madhyamaka, via the genuine understanding of shunyata and by a conscious application of this understanding to each present moment.

THE DISCIPLINE OF NO-DISCIPLINE

This brings us to the so-called 'discipline' angle. While this philosophy is not a form of spiritual or mystical idealism that requires a strenuous discipline to achieve some difficult and rare spiritual goal, such as proximity to God, or mystical experience, etcetera, this is not to say that it is easy in any ordinary sense. On the contrary, this approach is as disciplined in its way as any other. However, the nature of the discipline required is rather different, indeed unique. While other approaches may require a person to fight against temptation, combat desires, pray constantly, recite mantras, chant, yoga, rituals, purify the mind through fasting, austerities and the like, for example, perhaps even turning away from the world in monastic retreat, the Madhyamaka approach requires as crucial only one thing. The 'one thing needful' is to apply the ongoing discipline necessary to stop oneself backsliding into addiction to this or that fixated belief about reality.

The reason that this is difficult—in the sense of tricky to get the knack of it—is that the backsliding happens automatically and swiftly unless countered by a vigilant *awareness* together with a genuine *insight* into what is happening as it happens. The mind, it seems, is already conditioned biologically and by socialisation (and some would say also by karmic forces from past lives) to conceptually construct reality and become addicted to these constructs and their associated desires. The main point is that if we don't specifically act to remedy this, it automatically recurs. In other words, there is a kind of causal current that is carrying us in a certain direction. Unless we act to be free from the current, we will automatically be carried away by it and so get entangled in our delusions and cravings once again. *To do nothing about it is to fail*, for the current will carry us back in an instant.

Hence, a practice of insight-awareness is required: observing what one's mind is currently constructing in thought and projecting as reality, while also being critically aware of its voidance, that it is only a system of unfounded assumptions. Why base one's happiness on a system of unfounded assumptions? Why be so, well... gullible?

There seems to be little value in the practice of watchfulness or attentiveness if this is done by itself *without insight*. A person without insight might watch and attend, but if one does not know what one is watching for or attending to, and why, and if one does not have an understanding of what the mind is doing, then this watchfulness and attention may be of no use. What is needed is not just watchfulness or attention: one also needs the factor of insight or the application of what may be called in Buddhism 'right or skilful understanding'. This insight is the insight gained through learning about and fully comprehending shunyata. When the dialectic is fully appropriated and understood down to the bone, so to speak, so that it has become second nature, one can apply it readily and instantaneously: the readiness is all. The direct insight into voidance is a kind of condensed understanding of the whole dialectical process and its implications. The whole thing is comprehended in an instant and applied to each moment with increasing steadiness and assurance.

This requires mastery of the art of shunyata. Of course, such mastery, as in all rare arts, only comes through prolonged immersion in study of the matter and in constant practice—until practice makes perfect, as they say. So this might not come easily or in a short time for any particular person. However, on the other hand, we have to note this: the only way to develop this mastery in the future is to practice it in the present and *that* means to *let go* of everything here and now, *including all attempts to develop anything in the future*. For the very concept of the future, and any pursuit of future ideals, is also voided in the present moment of shunyata awareness. Well then: it seems that the only way to pursue shunyata is not to pursue shunyata—or anything else for that matter—but void everything and simply be (but not *as* anything!) in the voided moment. Hence: it is more a matter of just *being there*—of 'being nobody, going nowhere'—than of actually *pursuing* anything.[7] One is aimless in shunyata. There is nothing to pursue and no one to pursue it. That is perhaps the ultimate in being laidback!

This is a very unusual kind of discipline, because typically disciplines are about pursuing some ideal in the future. Indeed, we might even call it: the discipline of no-discipline. For here we are letting go of everything, including letting go of pursuits and goals. We just void everything, including time, seeking, and goals—even the sense of being a separate temporal self that has personal goals and ideals to pursue. Here is the thing: although it is a discipline, it is an incredibly relaxed discipline, if properly understood. As it is all about being *non-grasping*, obviously you don't have to grasp at or after anything. After all, if you are pursuing something in the future, that would just be another desire, another potential source of conflict and duhkha. Therefore, in this meditation you don't have to become anything, you don't have to attain anything or—if we may put it this way—the only thing you attain is non-attainment. For you void all ideas of attainment, and that is the attainment of non-attainment. Nothing to attain: what could be easier? All you have to do is be yourself—empty, just so. And because there is nothing to attain and no temporal pursuit, there is no conflict with what always already is: just so. You can just let everything be as voided, as non-dual, as unspeakable! Then there is no trouble, not even the trouble of having to attain enlightenment. Enough of that and everything else! Don't put yourself to any trouble!

In other words: chill out, relax, and stop agitating yourself for something. Just let it all go! Ah yes, that is it! It is all summed up in that little phrase: *letting go*. I mean to say, if non-attachment is the way and the cure, surely the only real practice worth anything is simple and direct—letting go, right here, right now. Everything else in Buddhism is decoration.

TWO TIERS OF TRUTH

Let us consider a glitch at this point, for it must somehow be resolved. It is this: the shunyata philosophy is a critical dialectic that reveals that no view of reality can be established as essentially true or right, or more true or right than any other view, such as a directly opposite view—'the opposite is also true!'—as an ancient sceptical saying goes. In effect, the critical dialectic results in a form of radical scepticism, or agnosticism, regarding all views or constructions of reality. It then advocates that we critically suspend all such thought-forms and so restore Existence Itself to its original purity as construction-free. It says we should do this because our disease in life is caused by our addiction to desires and pursuits, which in turn are caused by our addiction to constructions of reality. We should simply stop being so narrow-mindedly attached to any one view and become more open-minded; contemplating in openness (shunyata).

However, the following objection arises: 'If no view is more probable than any other, then the view that our suffering is caused by conceptual constructions—and will be eliminated with their elimination—cannot be said to be more probably true than any other view. For example, the view that our suffering is caused by brain chemicals, or by deep-rooted unconscious forces, as psychoanalysis says, or even by demons or gods or supernatural powers, as some cultures believe. Why then privilege a life of critically eliminating conceptual constructions and views? For this is itself a view. A view that we can liberate ourselves by eliminating views. Isn't there an inconsistency here?'

On the face of it, this seems like a good objection. The Madhyamaka philosophy may have successfully shown that all philosophical views of reality have inherent weak points and flaws, even that they are self-contradictory in some respects, and are therefore dubious—not something to cling to. However, it seems that the Madhyamaka is itself caught in a flaw or self-contradiction in holding to the view that it is beneficial to eliminate views. Is there an answer to this paradox?

The answer seems to be that the Madhyamaka advocates a kind of two-tier approach to life and truth. There is, on the one hand, what could be called the <u>ultimate level</u>. This is the pure shunyata-moment of awareness: the moment of radical deconstruction or meditative insight. From the standpoint of this consciousness, it is indeed the case that no view holds, not even the view that our suffering is caused by underlying views and that we should act with a view to eliminating views. Rather, there is at that moment of contemplation, a silent and judgement-free awareness of Existence Itself in all its immediacy and impenetrable mystery. There is an immediate stillness, an inward silence and non-dual emptiness.

However, the fact is, we do not live out our lives as merely contemplative beings. We also have to think and act in the world: make decisions, commit ourselves to this or that course and so pursue what *seems* to us at the time to be the best move to make. The shunyata insight cannot, in and of itself, determine our decisions, since it merely reveals the void and assumptive nature of all our decisions. So when it comes to action in the world we have to fall back on our more mundane ideas, beliefs, intuitions, experiences and feelings. At this point we are back at the <u>ordinary level</u> of language, thought, judgement and action. From the standpoint of shunyata, we realise, of course, that we could be completely wrong in whatever ordinary everyday judgements and decisions we make at the mundane level. We see that the opposite of them is also true, as it were. We see that whatever we say can be unsaid. We see that whatever judgements and decisions we make are merely provisional 'fallible commitments' (as we might put it) and that we are engaging in a way of life that could easily be a big mistake in the grand scheme of things (fundamentalist Islam could be correct, etcetera, who knows?)

Thus, there are two levels operating here: the *ultimate* contemplative level where we see through and void all judgement, and the *ordinary* level where we *must* make some kind of decision and engage in some kind of thought and action. The latter is indeed compelled. For there is no escaping it—logically, we must choose, for to not choose, or not commit ourselves, is itself a choice and a commitment (as Sartre, among others, points out).

However, it still might be urged the shunyata moment of awareness is not merely 'another tier or level coexisting with the ordinary level of thought and action,' but it actually *undermines* the ordinary level altogether, such that it becomes *impossible* to make decisions and act. For, it seems, we have no definite view of reality left to go on. In reply, we must say this: shunyata awareness only undermines everything within contemplation. That is, it generates awareness that things are voidable. However, it does not undermine everything when it comes to new action. For regardless of the shunyata awareness, we automatically have (for whatever ultimate reason, some form of conditioning perhaps) our spontaneous feelings and intuitions that such-and-such a judgement or course of action *seems* right or best to us at the time. These ordinary judgements based on 'seeming' are naturally reoccurring, although they are dubious, secondary, provisional, less-than-ultimate and not necessarily rational.

We say that these spontaneous intuitions and judgements arise 'for whatever reason' because, in fact, we cannot *know* what the ultimate reason or cause of them is. They *could* be caused by a rational response to the world being the way it is, by layers of self-deception, by natural biological factors, by cultural conditioning factors, or they *could* be caused by God or supernatural or karmic factors or even by other more mysterious factors, such as demonic or alien influences, as some cultures believed. From the standpoint of contemplative voidness, it is impossible to say what the causes are and no single theory of causes will be any more probably true than any other.

After this kind of realisation we can only accept such judgements tentatively and provisionally. They are just what *appears* or *seems* best to us at the time, we know not why. One goes along with them, but non-dogmatically, ironically, tongue-in-cheek, as it were. So, for instance, if it seems to you that your mental suffering is caused by fix- ated ideas and beliefs and that it can be dissolved by eliminating them, and you find that this view is appealing or seductive to you, you will probably act accordingly. You will do your shunyata practice, albeit with tongue-in-cheek. Such a feeling that the approach is worthwhile might arise as a result of thinking that one has had some success with it in the past, or due to hearing about others who have had some success, or due to the inherent logic of the argument, etc- etera. Or it might arise for some other reason we have no knowledge of (demonic interference, etcetera). For whatever reason it arises, if it arises, then, at the ordinary level of thought and action you will pro- bably decide that it is best to adopt this approach to life rather than some other. It will *seem* good. But one is also aware that it might not actually be good at all. One goes along with what *seems* good while acknowledging that this does not mean that it really *is* good. One could be completely wrong, after all. Maybe I am talking a lot of rub- bish here! Who knows? If I could get my tongue out of my cheek, maybe I would blow a raspberry at myself.

Let us call such spontaneous feelings and judgements that arise in us at the ordinary level of thought and action our personal in- tuitions. Then what we are saying is: when it comes to action in the world, we act on our personal intuitions at the time about what to do. We act, think, decide, speak and engage on the basis of what seems right, true or best at the time, in accordance with some ultimately dubious intuition. We are not attached to the intuition being right, for we don't know where these intuitions actually come from, only that we are currently having them.

The person who has shunyata awareness will be no different from the ordinary person in this respect: he or she will also act on spontaneous (ultimately dubious) personal intuitions. However, there will be this difference, that the ordinary person decides, acts, speaks, etcetera, on the basis of intuitions, and is not aware of them as voidable. On the contrary, the ordinary person takes them as well-founded, well-evidenced—as 'sound judgements' and the like—perhaps even as objectively and universally true judgements! Hence the person may even conclude everyone ought to judge as he or she does, and if they do not, they are somehow objectively in the wrong—perhaps sub-human, sub-rational or plain perverse, stupid, wicked or evil. In short, the person will be to some degree rigid and dogmatic and very likely rather intolerant too. Well, that is not uncommon.

The person who has shunyata awareness, however, will not be dogmatic. He or she will be aware that personal intuitions are not reliable, that they are voidable, arising as they do in the mind and heart for who knows what reasons. He or she will also be aware that there is no way of deciding objectively or ultimately between the different intuitions that different people have. We can only go on our own intuitions. And if we offer some point of view to others, we can only hope that their intuitions are not so far removed from ours that they will see some value in our point of view and maybe act accordingly.

We must say now, the view that the shunyata approach to life is best, is itself merely an intuition, and that the argument our actions and decisions are based only on intuitions is only another intuition. Therefore, one cannot even be dogmatic about the value or validity of the shunyata philosophy as compared to others. It will appeal to some people only insofar as it happens to appeal to their intuitions. If it does, then they will meditate on voidance and get whatever benefit it may have for them. All that can be suggested is that people try the philosophy and practice to test its value in experience. That is, if it suits their current intuitions to do so!

Finally then: in the moment of shunyata contemplation we restore Existence Itself to its immediacy voided of concepts, ideas, judgements, evaluations, etcetera. We simply are just so; restored to *pure
is-ness* and not dualistically separate from the general is-ness. We let
go of all ontological distinctions, including so-called alterity: otherness. We tend to find that in this letting go and letting be in voidance
peace gathers of itself (or so it seems). Greater wellbeing arises (or so
it seems). Then—at the level of ordinary thinking, discussing, eval-
uating, deciding and acting—we act on our own dubious personal
intuitions as best we can, as they naturally occur to us, yet without
taking them dogmatically to be true or valid. They are, as it were,
only tentative projections into the vast unknown. No need to take
them too seriously! No need to take them as final or fixed or ultimate!
Hence, they need not get in the way of our basic open-mindedness or
openness.

The ordinary everyday world of ontological divisions is seen
through at any moment as merely a provisional construction of one's
mind and language; our best guess, a stab in the dark, a hunch. No
more than that. One tends to take it more lightly, as potentially a deception, a veil, or a dance of illusion (*Maya* or *Lila*). We can be more
playful and humorous, because we don't take the world or the self so
seriously any more; they are not given truths and set realities. Others
may have their own intuitions about self and reality and they are just
as likely to be as right (or wrong) as we are. There are no grounds for
making a definitive judgement; hence no grounds for taking a dogmatic, superior or self-righteous attitude. It may all be much ado
about nothing (as Shakespeare often seems to suggest).

Perhaps we will find that a more peaceful, serene, easygoing, acc-
ommodating and tolerant approach to life tends to develop in us, in
a natural way, as a result of this approach and shunyata practice. Who
knows? One can but try it and see how it goes. I mean, one can
always regard it as just an experiment, or hobby or a curious game to
play. It's no big deal. I mean, what is a 'big deal' in this voidable reality? If 'fundamentally, not one thing exists,' as the Zen Master Hui-

Neng (638–713) says, then what's the fuss?[8] Seeing it thus, one can relax, let go and enjoy *what is* (whatever it is) in all its wondrous beauty and profound mystery. The so-called discipline of meditation becomes 'easy, so easy' then—a letting go into the non-dual and nameless Way of what is. Very pleasant and agreeable to do, so no problem doing it!

INTO EVERY LIFE A LITTLE ZEN MUST FALL?[9]

Zen Buddhism is based on the Madhyamaka tradition and so should reflect it. But just as there are at least two main interpretations of the shunyata doctrine (as represented by Murti and Streng) so there have been at least two main interpretations of Zen.

In the 'golden age' of Zen in China during the T'ang Dynasty (600–900 AD) when Zen was called Ch'an, these two interpretations were represented by the Northern School (or 'gradual' school) and by the Southern School (or 'sudden' school). The Northern School seems to have adopted a view akin to Murti's. It seems to have taught that the ultimate is some kind of mystical experience revealing that reality is an absolute unity. Consequently, it taught a practice of 'gradual enlightenment,' namely, that through a gradual approach of constant spiritual practice and purification (constantly wiping the mind clean of thoughts in sitting meditation or zazen) we will eventually attain to a mystical experience or satori. Only then will we be enlightened and only then do we 'escape from the wheel of karma and rebirth,' as they say.[10]

The Southern School, on the other hand, seems to have taken an approach rather more like Streng's. Here it was taught that the best way is to have an immediate insight into the voidance of all reality constructions and so let go of everything, lock, stock and barrel. If so, enlightenment has to be sudden and immediate in the present. Hence, it is *not* a gradual or graduated process of acquiring merits in various stages, of reducing bad karma, and slowly building a capacity for some kind of supposedly mystical revelation or enlightenment in the future. One lets go of that pursuit along with everything else.

The Northern (gradual) School and Murtian type of interpretation tend to dominate how Zen is understood and presented in
the West these days. Perhaps this has come about because of the influential writings of D. T. Suzuki (1870–1966), who seems to have
been addicted to a dogmatic truth that everything is an absolute One
and that this needs to be known by way of a mystical illumination.
That Suzuki has misrepresented the Ch'an of the T'ang Dynasty has
been argued by the scholar Hu Shih in a paper published in the
journal *Philosophy East and West* (April 1953) entitled 'Ch'an (Zen)
Buddhism in China: Its History and Method.'

In this paper, Hu Shih highlights just how radical the Ch'an Masters were in rejecting the traditional Buddhist religious concepts: such
as the doctrine of karma, rebirth, worship of the Buddha, the doctrine
of Nirvana as some future state, acquisition of merits, a gradual approach to enlightenment and the view that reality is a mystical unity.
They spent a lot of time and energy trying to liberate the minds of
their disciples from being addicted to such views. In this it seems they
were being true to the shunyata teaching, simply applying it in notably novel, down-to-earth and dramatic ways. Anyone exhibiting
addiction to a view was liable to get his ears pulled, or get whacked,
or kicked down the stairs and so on.

As Hu Shih puts it, the goal of the exercise was to achieve self-
emancipation; to free the mind from emotional clinging to dogmatic
views and grasping at reality in concepts. Then, through this emancipation from dogma, one could emancipate the heart from its emotional clinging to the various objects of desire. Hu Shih concluded
that Zen is not something that is essentially mystical or irrational or
'altogether beyond the ken of human understanding,' as Suzuki said
it was.[11] Rather, it is somewhat more like a form of critical therapy
that aims to liberate people from their addictions and hang-ups by
emancipating them from the conceptual and emotional 'prisons of
conviction' in which they are caught. We are, in effect, our own worst
enemies, for it is this enthralment to our own mind—the believing,

desiring, chattering, monkey-mind—that blocks us from being free
and at peace here and now. If we can suspend the influence of this
monkey-mind in any meditative moment of insight, we can be restored in openness (shunyata) to Existence Itself. And therein lies
peace, it seems.

How to practice this? Well, you don't have to light a candle or sit
down cross-legged and pretend to be an immovable stone Buddha
without a thought. It is more like this. Suppose one day you happen
to come across this funny little guy with unkempt hair standing all

alone on a soap box at speaker's corner in the park pontificating on
and on about something, finger in the air, like a slightly crazed-look-
ing demagogue or guru, and suppose you happen to be in a fairly
quiet, confident, alert, amused, sceptical frame of mind that day.
There is no way you are going to buy into the stuff he is saying. You
just watch and listen with a kind of mild curiosity, noting his idio-
syncrasies and assumptions. So unperturbed are you that you don't
even feel any particular need to answer him back or jump into a debate with him, or to get him to shut up. He can rant on if he wants;
the stuff just rolls off you like water off a duck's back. You can see
through it straightaway, see how dubious and void it is, so it causes
you no trouble or upset or harm at all.

Suppose that after a bit of ranting, seeing how unaffected you are
by it, the funny little guy gradually runs out of steam, out of words
and momentum. He just slows down all by himself and goes quiet.
You haven't had to force him to go quiet. It's more like your refusal to
buy into his rant makes him go quiet quite naturally.

It is a bit like this with our own so-called monkey-mind. You
don't have to do anything special, like get into some fancy oriental
posture or mumble some exotic chants. You don't have to act on the
mind, or do anything to the mind at all, which, after all, is just doing
what minds naturally do. All you do is just watch and listen with
critical intelligence, with insight-awareness. Then it can rant on all it
wants and it will be like water off a duck's back to you. And so, precisely by *not* arguing or struggling with the mind, not agitating it

(which just stirs up the mud, as it were) but rather by giving the mind free reign while *not* being fooled and sucked in by its thoughts and desires, one can let it go naturally quiet, all by itself. As it tends to do, if one stops feeding it with new inputs of the same sort, that is, with yet more thoughts and desires, such as to attain enlightenment before Christmas and so forth.

It may take a little time, because after all, the little monkey has built up some momentum. But gradually it tends to run out of steam by itself if one doesn't try and force any particular issue or outcome. Suppose it does not run out of steam in ten minutes or before Christmas? Well, okay then. Void any bad judgements you have about that as well!

What is being applied here is nothing but shunyata: voidance. The mind rants and one renders the rant null and void: harmless, weightless, suspended, empty—shunyata. It raves, you chill. Very likely it will soon calm down. Then it's nice to just sit in that wonderful silence and maybe... contemplate the beauty of the rose.

That's all. There is no trouble in life if we don't fabricate any.

Meditation then is quite easy, quite pleasant and quite natural—not forced, not artificial, not mystical.

How to meditate? Whatever comes up—void it!

Who then are you?

2

RADICAL SCEPTICISM AND SUSPENSE

No more likelihood that this is true than that.
— ancient sceptical saying

THROUGHOUT THE HISTORY of Western philosophy there has been a dynamic between the more 'constructive efforts' in philosophy—that is, people trying to create metaphysical systems, explanations of reality, trying to grasp reality in concepts—and on the other hand, just as many movements dedicated to 'deconstructing' those systems again, almost as soon as they have been created.

We have had a dialectical movement since the earliest to the present time of creation then destruction. In the process it seems that the more sceptical movements always tend to win the day. A new belief-system gets created by a Plato (427–347 BC), a Kant (1724–1804), a Schopenhauer (1788–1860), etcetera, and then in the next decade or two, other thinkers arise to probe and question those belief-systems, even to poke fun at them. They have generally been able to show the systems cannot stand because they have various fundamental difficulties and flaws. It has got to the point nowadays that there are very few philosophers left who seriously think it is possible to construct a complete metaphysical system or ultimate explanation of reality and most modern philosophers have abdicated from that task.

There have been two main types of reaction. The one most common to the Anglo-American philosophical world is to give up the idea of discussing metaphysics directly at all and instead concentrate on analysis of language. *Linguistic analysis* became the big thing in the first half of the twentieth century. Meanwhile, on the Continent, *existentialism* (and later on, postmodernism) became the big thing, as philosophers attempted to make something interesting out of this situation where true systems no longer seem to be a possibility (we will look at existentialism in detail in the next chapter).

We might wonder why it is that scepticism tends to win out in these dialectical battles. But before we look at that, let us pose a fundamental question: What is knowledge and who has knowledge, if anyone?

THE QUESTION OF KNOWLEDGE

This is, of course, a very important question, because it has all sorts of ramifications. Political ramifications, for instance, because knowledge is power as they say. If some people can make their self-serving claims to be knowledgeable stick, this would give them authority, prestige and power over many others in society. In the Indian tradition, for example, if it is widely believed and accepted the priestly caste of Brahmins have the essential knowledge, then the Brahmins will gain a certain amount of power accordingly, for example the power to determine the nature of reality and society, to lay down rules for the caste system, to prescribe values and so on. They will become the arbiters of the basic beliefs and value standards for that society. So it has been a very important issue to decide who has knowledge.

Before we can consider the question, 'who has knowledge?' we obviously have to consider, 'what is knowledge?' because before we can decide who has it, we have to know what it is, what constitutes knowledge, so we can recognise if a particular person or group has it or not. Philosophers have seen the importance of this question. Accordingly, that branch of study called *epistemology* came to the fore. Epistemology is derived from the ancient Greek word *episteme* meaning knowledge, and that part of philosophy studies knowledge: what it really is, how we get it, what the difference is between knowledge and belief.

Many would regard epistemology as the logical starting point for all human thought, for it seems that until or unless we decide this 'question of knowledge' there is hardly much point going on to other issues, since it could be doubted whether people have any real knowledge or authority to speak about them. So 'what is knowledge?' is a very fundamental question in all our reasoning and believing about life and reality.

It seems rather silly, then, when people react to this, as they often do, by saying, 'Well, this is a very impractical or airy-fairy type of pursuit and we should just get on with the practical business of life instead of doing all this philosophising'. That seems silly because the question is: What *is* the practical business of life? Do we know what we *should* we be doing? What *is* life all about? How can we decide *that* until we have decided what knowledge is? The question of what knowledge is and what we know (if anything) surely has a certain priority because without this, how can we know what we are supposed to be doing in life and what is or is not practical? People assume too quickly that it is sensible and pragmatic to get on with life in the sense of pursuing their businesses, their daily affairs, their ordinary way of life, etcetera. But that presupposes that they already have some reliable knowledge of what reality really is, what the meaning of life is, what goals to aim for, and so on. They are making some big assumptions there before they start. So it is quite a *practical* question, when you think about it, to raise this issue about what knowledge is and whether we have any. If so, then philosophy itself is an eminently practical subject, not airy-fairy or irrelevant.

What have philosophers had to say about epistemology, knowledge and belief, down through the ages? First of all, they have noticed that we make *claims* to have knowledge but we don't make *claims* to have belief. Why is that? Why does knowledge have this notion of *claim* associated with it? It suggests there is something rather special about knowledge. It seems that a claim to knowledge requires some sort of *justification* to back it up, whereas this is not the case for belief. People can believe all sorts of things on the flimsiest of grounds and that is just a psychological state that they are in. This is okay. But if they go on to claim knowledge of something—perhaps because knowledge is so much connected with prestige, power, and authority, hence typically is self-serving—we want to carefully test the grounds for the claim by asking: What warrant does the person have for making that claim to have knowledge?

So claims, and good grounds for the claims, are very important in connection with knowledge, not so important in connection with belief. Also, if people claim to know something is true, as being 'the truth,' this seems to imply that, if the claim to have knowledge is justified, then what they claim to know really is true. That is, a proper claim to knowledge would imply the truth of the thing said to be known, for we cannot rightly claim to know something that is, in fact, false. For example, I can't say I know that Sydney is the capital of Australia, when in fact it isn't.

So, first of all, genuine knowledge seems to imply the truth of that which is claimed to be known, and knowledge differs from belief in this respect, because obviously people can believe all sorts of things that are, in fact, false. Secondly, knowledge seems to presuppose belief—that is, if I say that I *know* Canberra is the capital of Australia this would imply I also *believe* it. For it would be very odd for me to say, 'I *know* that Canberra is the capital of Australia but I don't *believe* it'. This seems to be the case because knowledge is more stringent than belief. Typically, if we have sufficient warrant to make a claim to knowledge this would be enough also to establish a state of belief in our minds.

So far, then, we have the idea that knowledge implies *true belief*, we have a belief about something and this belief is true. Is that all though? Philosophers and logicians have generally said this is not sufficient. For example, a person might say, 'I know that the next horse to win the Melbourne Cup will be called such-and-such.' Somebody may ask, 'Well, how do you know that?' and the person replies, 'Well, I had this dream the other night.' We would probably regard that as rather weak evidence on which to base a claim to knowledge, especially if the person has no prior history of having prophetic dreams. We would feel justified in questioning the validity of a claim to knowledge here and would probably be unwise to place any money on it.

 So we see that we need some kind of good, high-quality evidence to justify or warrant a claim to knowledge. Let's add a new twist to it though and try this: as it turns out, the winning horse in the Melbourne Cup is indeed such-and-such, the very horse it was said would win. Now let's assume that the person was *sincere* when he or she said, 'I know that such-and-such will win the Melbourne Cup.' The person really did *believe* that horse would win, and thus had belief. Secondly, the belief *was* true, because, in fact, the horse *did* win the Melbourne Cup. So the person had a true belief. Do we conclude then that the person also had knowledge? No, because the basis for it seems so flimsy, not the sort of grounds we generally accept as justifying a claim to knowledge. We are likely to dismiss it as knowledge, because it could have just been a coincidence or a fluke that the person happened to have that dream and came up with the right horse.

 To sum up, such considerations have led philosophers and logicians to define proper knowledge as *justified true belief*.

One may begin to see a problem arising from this though. *Justified true belief* is a little vague on the question of what constitutes justification. What is *sufficient* justification in the case of making a claim to knowledge? That has been the main bone of contention down through the ages with regard to people who have claimed to have real knowledge about things.

Someone might say, for instance, 'I know that God exists'. You might ask, 'Well, how do you know this? What is the basis, what is the warrant for this claim? Why should I believe it?' etcetera. The person may say something like, 'Well, I hear God's voice in the bath.

When I am in the bath I hear God talking to me, and so God exists'
(a student actually said this to me once). However, this seems a very
weak basis for a claim to knowledge. After all, schizophrenics often
hear voices. The source of the voice is often not what the person takes
it to be. The source could well lie in the person's own unconscious
mind, for example. So hearing a voice would not be sufficient basis
for claiming to know that a God exists.

Or suppose somebody says, 'Well, I know God exists because the
Bible tells me so.' Again this seems weak, because questions can be
raised about the authority of the Bible, or it can be pointed out that
there are other holy scriptures—the Qur'an, the Vedas, etcetera—that
say different things, giving a different picture of the metaphysical situation than the Bible. Or questions might be raised about the internal
coherence of the Bible, and so on. Reference to the Bible would not
be taken by most philosophers as being a sufficient basis to make a
claim to have knowledge of the real existence of a God.

Similar arguments can be brought up against, not just voices, but
dreams, visions, spiritual experiences, mystical experiences, etcetera.
Similar problems apply: one can always raise questions about whether the experience is really an experience of something that is objectively real and true. After all, it might just be some kind of hallucination or projection from the person's own unconscious mind. Or the
person may simply have the wrong *interpretation* of the experience
and what it really means or implies about the nature of reality.

This type of questioning has generally led people, especially in
modern times, to be rather sceptical of religious claims to knowledge.
So they have said that knowledge is not possible or appropriate in the
area of religion. And even many religious people these days would
accept that. They would fall back on the notion of *faith* instead and
would say, 'Well, okay, you can't have true knowledge in the area of
religion. Therefore, what's needed is some kind of leap of faith.' They
have abdicated from the idea of establishing religious knowledge.
They see that there are sufficient rational grounds for doubt and they
fall back on the notion of a personal leap of faith instead.

Certainly many modern people, and the majority of modern philosophers, would reject the idea that there can be real knowledge in
the area of religion. So that has led many people to be sceptical in that
area. Many modern philosophers then say: 'Okay, we can't have
knowledge in that area, but we can have knowledge in some other
area; namely, in the area of what can be empirically verified in a properly scientific way.' They can point out evidence seems to be stronger
and more convincing if we are talking about something that can be
publicly and empirically tested in repeatable ways, and also if it
connects well with the rest of our body of so-called knowledge. So it
has been suggested that verification by empirical means and the coherence of certain ideas and propositions with other ideas and propositions we accept and that have been verified in various ways, will be
what properly constitutes true knowledge. They say this is our best
route to knowledge.

Many people, and many philosophers in the twentieth century,
are what we might call 'limited sceptics'. They are rather sceptical
about metaphysical, religious, or spiritual issues, but they are not sceptical about whatever can be established scientifically through repeated public testing. They believe that only science can supply true
knowledge. However, we find that in the history of Western philosophy there have been sceptics who have been much more radical
and extreme in their scepticism than this.

They pose the troublesome question: How can we prove or disprove the existence of any kind of supernatural being or power that
lies beyond the realm of empirical evidence? It would seem that we
could neither prove nor disprove something like this by the empirical
evidence. Even most scientists and scientifically minded philosophers
would accept that one must remain *agnostic* with regard to questions
like that. Hence, they are accepting that it is at least *possible* that such
a supernatural being exists—or several such beings, for all we know.
However, if that is admitted as a possibility, then it logically follows
that the possibility also exists that this being or these beings could be
constantly interfering with things that happen in our ordinary realm

of empirical experience. That cannot be ruled out now.

Science often claims to be without presuppositions, but it surely makes one here if it assumes that the scientific empirical experience ✓ is *non-deceptive*; that is, that nothing could be interfering with it from a spiritual or transcendental dimension. One is surely engaging in an assumption if one takes it for granted that the ordinary emprical reality of the senses is the sole or final court of appeal, as it were, or if one takes it as being veridical in itself, and that we *can* and *should* base all our so-called knowledge only on that. For there is this perplexing possibility that supernatural beings, unknown forces and so on, may exist and could well be interfering with our empirical experiences and experiments. I mean, for all we know.

Consider a couple of examples: supposing I was a fundamentalist type of Christian who believes in God and also the Devil. After all, the Devil is talked about in the Gospels so if one accepts the Gospels and God one might accept the Devil as well. Supposing we are considering a particular issue like, say, the Shroud of Turin. Some people believe that Jesus was wrapped in this piece of cloth when he was placed in the tomb. There is an image of a crucified man on the cloth, and it has puzzled some people as to how it has got there because it doesn't seem to be painted on, etcetera.

However, eventually carbon-dating tests were carried out on small pieces of the cloth in three different laboratories and it was agreed the cloth could not be earlier than the twelfth century or thereabouts. Therefore, it could not be the cloth Jesus was wrapped in. However, I have met and talked with some strongly believing Christians who are not in the least fazed by this because they have a simple expedient. They can claim that we are living in a situation dominated by spiritual 'principalities and powers,' as they say. From their point of view, reality consists of a battle between these powers and, if so, it is certainly possible that any scientific experiment conducted, especially in the area of religion, can and probably will be disturbed and distorted by these powers. So no matter how many times you test something like the Shroud of Turin scientifically, whatever evidence you get could be dismissed as a deception because it has been interfered with by some evil and deceiving power. Or perhaps, they may say by God, as a test of our faith. This test might separate the sheep from the goats. If you are a *true* believer and you have *real* faith then you will stick to your beliefs even in the face of scientific or empirical evidence to the contrary and so on.

So they have a rather closed picture of things and it is impossible to actually break into that circle or argue against it. If you accept their premises then the rest of what they believe follows from that. Meanwhile, if you accept the scientific premise—the starting point being the veracity of empirical evidence—then everything else follows from that. But the question is: Why accept those *first premises* when we cannot establish them independently? We just have to just start from *assuming* them to be true although their truth can't be proved. So both science and religion begin to appear like two closed circles that can never really, in the last analysis, connect or seriously argue against one another. Science, for instance, can never disprove anything for the religious person who wishes to dispute the veracity of 'empirical evidence' as such, since all the reasoning in science is based on the premise that 'empirical evidence' is non-deceptively valid and the ultimate court of appeal.

Another example is the creationism issue. Now there *are* some religious people who call themselves 'creation scientists'. That is, they try and argue on *scientific grounds* that the world was created some seven thousand years ago. As they are arguing on scientific grounds their arguments are rather feeble and unpersuasive, because scientists can easily debate the scientific evidence they bring up. They bring up some dubious scientific claims. However, there are other creationists who don't buy into the scientific argument at all. They simply say that the world was created about seven thousand years ago and all the empirical evidence that suggests that it is far older than this was also created seven thousand years ago. Therefore, when you stop and think about it, one realises that there is actually no way to *disprove* that the world was created seven thousand years ago. Because whatever so-called 'empirical evidence' you point to (fossils in rocks, etcetera) was simply created seven thousand years ago.

So again, we have two closed circles that won't meet, two separate wheels spinning that don't really connect. One cannot disprove the other or even properly *engage* with the other. It all depends on what initial premises you wish to adopt. Religious people may choose to adopt the Bible, for example, as their sole starting point—their supreme authority and source of evidence—and anything that conflicts with the Bible would therefore be seen as something dubious, perhaps even demonic, or so they will say. There the conversation ends.

TOWARD RADICAL SCEPTICISM

We should note this very important point: if we appeal to empirical evidence to prove the validity of empirical evidence this is obviously a case of *arguing in a circle* and *begging the question* as to whether empirical evidence is veridical or not. It *already assumes* the non-deceptiveness of empirical evidence as such. Similar problems arise if you attempt to justify the validity of reason itself by using reason. Again, you will be arguing in a circle. Or if you attempt to validate memory by appealing to memories: again you will be arguing in a circle. We always have to start from some premise or other that is simply accepted as true from the very first, but without any proof, in order to build our argument from there. However, if the very first premise of the system, on which all the rest depends, is without proof then the system as a whole is without proof. In short, it's a dubious enterprise from beginning to end.

This has been recognised by existentialists and others, for example, Friedrich Nietzsche (1844–1900). Nietzsche spoke about how underlying all logic, all reasoning, all philosophy, stands *evaluation*: the choice to *value* some starting point as being authoritative for you.[1] For instance, it might be the Bible, or the faculty of human reason, or empirical evidence and verification, or personal experience, or intuition, etcetera. So *evaluation*, for Nietzsche, seemed to be much more fundamental than even so-called facts or so-called empirical proof or evidence. Evaluation seemed to him to be more fundamental because one has to first of all value and choose a method: a certain way of life and of thinking that involves a set of initial principles or first premises that you can't prove are true without arguing in a circle.

Existentialists also speak of the priority of our fallible existential commitments. If we commit ourselves existentially to the scientific method and view of reality, so-called scientific truths will follow from that, while if we commit ourselves existentially to the mystical method and view of reality then other so-called truths will follow from that, and so on. The choice to create a way of life for ourselves —or a meaning and direction in life—is what comes first and is really fundamental, the existentialists say, rather than so-called evidence, reason, logic or facts. Some choice of evaluation comes first, because we have to decide for ourselves what will *count* as *good* evidence, or what will count as evidence *for us personally*. And for all we know, we could be deceived in that initial choice of a meaning to life and method of inquiry: we could be going wrong right from the start.

This talk about the possibility of deception may remind us of René Descartes (1596–1650), the French philosopher who is well known for his sceptical reflections in his famous *Meditations*. There is an argument in Descartes' *Meditations* that is probably the shortest and quickest route to complete scepticism. That is where he suggests that there is indeed a possibility—for we can neither prove it nor disprove it—that there exists a God or supernatural being who is, in fact, a kind of evil being or a deceptive being. He says at one point: '...a God might have perhaps given me such a nature as that I should be deceived, even respecting the matters that appeared to me the most evidently true'.[2]

Now, when people think of God they tend to blindly assume from the first that God is good, hence trustworthy. However, if God is particularly devilish She would, of course, like to fool us. She might fool us into believing that we can trust our human senses and human rea-

son, we can trust our personal intuitions, or we can trust that whatever appears self-evidently true to us actually is true—when in fact,
all is utterly false. Such a trickster God might also like to fool us about
Her revelations and Her moral goodness, and so trick us into thinking She is worth believing and worshipping, because then She could
completely seduce us down the wrong path altogether. For instance,
She could trick us into believing that we can trust Her self-des-
criptions and promises about the next life, etcetera. But in fact this
God might be complete liar for all we know. How then could we believe anything that a being claiming to be God says or does or promises? It seems we cannot. For instance, perhaps this being called
God reserves a special place in hell for all those people who believe
in Him—or is it Her?

Therefore, there is very real possibility that if there is a God it
could be a deceiving God. But if *that* is the case then it must logically
follow that *whatever* we think or believe or intuit about the nature of
life and reality, no matter how certain it seems to us to be, could be a
complete deception created in our minds by this God. Therefore,
while we all must have beliefs, of course, in order to function, we cannot claim we have *justified true beliefs*. For we don't know what is reliable or true in our beliefs: there could be a comprehensive deception
going on, for all we know, since there is no way to prove or disprove
this. Therefore, as knowledge requires justified true belief, we cannot
claim to have any knowledge at all. In sum: all human knowledge is
undermined by the logical possibility that we could be radically deceived in the small sphere of what we think we know by something
from the bigger sphere of what we don't know.

Note that, in this way of thinking, any strong feelings of confidence or assurance we have that our beliefs about reality *are* correct
constantly fail to actually *prove* that they are. Feelings of assurance and
confidence do not prove anything. Obviously there are lots of people
who have very strong feelings of assurance and confidence that they
have met the Lord, for example. They may or may not be correct, but
their feelings of confidence do not prove the truth of the matter.

Likewise, if we too have strong feelings of confidence about our ideas of reality then this also would *not prove* that the ideas are true or correct. We could be mistaken in our feelings of assurance, for we don't even know from whence they originate or what is ultimately causing them. We are just aware we have them here and now, but we do not know how or why. In particular, we do not know if they are coming from a reliable source and hence, we don't know they are reliable. But if we don't know they are reliable, we are not justified in claiming them as a source of knowledge rather than deception. Hence, we do not have justified true beliefs. If so, there is no knowledge.

Going back to Descartes, he did eventually come to the conclusion that, yes, he could doubt virtually everything. After all, he could even be dreaming. He realised that when dreaming he has sometimes felt *very strongly* that some things are true and real only to later awaken and discover that they are not. Therefore, any extremely strong feeling of assurance we currently have that we are not dreaming simply *fails to prove* that we are not dreaming. Indeed, we could even be *dreaming* that we have a strong feeling of confidence that we are not dreaming! We could be dreaming that we are not in a dream! How could one even begin to disprove such a possibility? It seems impossible to do so.

So what we are experiencing right here, right now, could be a dream, for all we know. We might also remember that some people when hypnotised or mad see or do some very complex things that are not actually real, etcetera—and we could be in that state too. Some modern philosophers have gone so far as to raise the possibility that we could be just a *brain in a vat* being stimulated by electrodes to have an experience, somewhat similar to the situation in the movie, The Matrix.[3] Indeed, we could perceive and believe that we are in a material body, and that we are physical beings, but we might not be at all. Idealists claim, after all, that there is only mind and its perceptions. This is logically possible, and may be true, for all we know. No one yet has been able to disprove it. Rather, people just tend to ignore it. But that won't do in philosophy.

Descartes eventually got to the point of thinking that the only thing he could really be sure about was his own personal existence here and now. Anything outside of immediate experience would be to some extent *speculative*. So he reached his famous *cogito ergo sum* argument: 'I think, therefore I am'. All he could be sure about, he thought, was his own existence here and now as the one who was thinking these thoughts—his reasoning being that, if he doubts everything else, then at least he must exist as the doubter of all these things. So he must exist, at least here and now, as the thinker of these thoughts, or as the doubter.

However, some philosophers after Descartes—for example, Nietzsche—have said he was being a bit rash in making that assumption.[4] After all, how can we be sure that there is even a *self*—a persistent I, as a causal ego, or an agent, that is the source of the thinking or doubting process? This is quite a pertinent consideration in a Buddhist context, of course, because there are many Buddhists who deny the reality of the self or a personal ego as some kind of persisting agent in time, some kind of separate self-subsisting entity that creates or causes thoughts, or that wills and initiates actions. If we say there is, this is just an unproven assumption, because it is just as likely that there isn't—for all we know.

Nietzsche and others have proposed the idea that thoughts just appear in the mind for underlying causal reasons—e.g., physiological or chemical reasons. Neuro-chemical activity in the brain might be producing the thoughts: therefore, 'we,' as so-called selves or egos, are not actually creating or doing or controlling the thinking. At the very most 'we' are simply witnessing the thinking as it happens in our minds (or rather in our brains) but 'we' do not actually cause it. Similarly, when it comes to willing, when it comes to action, people tend to assume we are the agents who actually cause and will things to happen, but it may be that things just happen, as it were, *through us* rather than *by* us.

So this kind of reflection has led to the interminable debate between the issue of freewill and determinism: whether human beings have any freewill at all or whether all our actions are determined by natural causes, a whole series of them that are interconnected with all the other natural causes in the environment. Perhaps everything is interconnected in a complex web of natural causes? If so, our sense of separate selfhood is simply an illusory effect within this whole system of causes.

Philosophers have been arguing about that one for centuries and they have never been able to come to a definite conclusion about it. Nevertheless, the topic can't easily be dismissed, because it has some very important practical implications. In general it seems most people want to cling onto the idea of freewill so as to be able to hold other people accountable and morally responsible for their actions. That is important in courts of law when you are trying to decide whether a person is responsible and consequently punishable. The determinist thesis, on the other hand, seems to undermine our conventional concept of justice, because if a person does not have any freewill and is entirely the product of natural causes, then nobody is responsible for their actions at all and it seems a bit unfair, therefore, to punish them for things they cannot help but do, given their whole natural makeup, etcetera.

So that argument has been quite important, has very practical moral importance as well, but still nobody has been able to decide the matter one way or the other. So we see that there are important questions that can be asked about whether the self exists or not as a real persistent and separate entity, or as a real being with a coherent self-identity, or whether it exists as a causal agent, whether it has freewill, and whether it is a proper object for praise or for blame, punishment or desert. We should realise we are skating on very thin ice when we make our everyday assumptions and assertions about such matters.

Also, it has been asked: If Descartes doubts everything except his immediate existence here and now, what sort of self is he referring to when he says 'I think, therefore I am'? He can't really be referring to the self as some kind of continuous self-subsistent being that exists through time, since he is questioning everything outside the present moment of experience. The idea of himself as some kind of personal persisting identity would be something subject to his own Cartesian doubts; e.g., doubts about the validity of memory and the past.

On this point about doubt with regard to time and the past: the philosopher Bertrand Russell (1872–1970) once raised the point that, 'There is no logical impossibility in the hypothesis that the world sprang into being five minutes ago, exactly as it then was, with a population that "remembered" a wholly unreal past.'[5] How can we know or prove that the world existed more than five minutes ago? This is similar to the issue we raised before about everything being created seven thousand years ago. It doesn't really matter whether we are talking about six or seven thousand years ago, or about six or seven minutes ago. The same argument applies. For all we know, everything could have come into existence a few minutes ago complete with all the empirical or other evidence that suggests the world is much older than this. This will include all of us who have so-called 'memories' of a world that existed more than a few minutes ago. Of course, we all have the same sort of memories in regard to the past, so we all agree more-or-less about it. However, that doesn't prove the world existed more than a few minutes ago. It only proves that there is a correlation between our so-called memories *now*. The deception, after all, could be a comprehensive and shared one.

So we cannot, in fact, prove by any means at all that the world existed more than a few minutes ago—which is quite a staggering thought actually! We don't have to make it five minutes. Let's make it two minutes. Two minutes is even more staggering!

In this way of radical doubting we can arrive at different versions of what is called *solipsism*. The main kind of solipsism was the Cartesian solipsism in his situation of 'I think, therefore I am'. He was not even able to prove that anybody else existed, because he could only contact people through his own perception of them. So all he knew existed was his perception of people. He could not know that those other people had minds, because he never directly contacted their minds. After all, we only see the outward form of people, their actions, speech and so forth. For all we know, they may not have minds in themselves.

Solipsism is the theory that only 'I' exist, that there is no real world out there in itself, only my perception or dream of one. We can have an even more extreme form, the 'solipsism of the present moment,' as it were, where we cannot be sure that anything other than the self of the present moment exists (which is not really a self at all then, in any usual sense of the word). If so, our ideas of things outside or beyond the immediate experience of the present moment are merely speculative. As we saw, we can doubt the reality of the continuous self in time, the existence of the self as a personal and temporal self-identity. Perhaps only this present moment, with its here-and-now content of experience, whether we call it perception, sensation, thought, feeling, consciousness, or a dream, is all that exists.

All this doubting and questioning may remind us of an idea expressed way back in the beginning of the history of Western philosophy in connection with Socrates (469–399 BC); namely, what the Delphic Oracle probably meant when it said that Socrates was the wisest man in Greece. It was said he was the wisest because he was the only person who realised that he knew nothing, whereas everybody else thought that they knew something. Therefore, he was a step ahead of them on that point, a little bit wiser than they in realising all that we can really say is that we know nothing at all.

But can we even say this? Can we say anything at all? Our language affects how we think and what we say about reality, how we structure reality in thought and experience. If we had a different type of language, with a grammatical structure more adapted to expressing processes, we would probably think of reality in terms of processes. Our English language is structured through nouns and verbs, so we tend to think in terms of things or agents that act. We look for ultimate entities such as atoms, particles or egos. If we had a language of process, more like the Apache Indian or Chinese language, we might think in terms of ephemeral events and connected processes as the ultimate nature of reality, rather than things or agents.

Not only that, but if memory is questionable, our ability to remember and properly label or identify things would be questionable. A correct use of language depends on a correct use of memory. Language, after all, could be an internal part of that aforementioned 'dubious dream' we may be having. If so, even recognising, describing, and conceptualising things in the present moment would be a questionable enterprise. How do we know we are identifying and speaking things correctly, using the words correctly, or forming the sentences correctly? That deceptive God may be fooling us into thinking that we know what we mean. How then do we know that we are properly forming our thoughts and that they are not just a jumble of nonsense verses that falsely appear to us to be sensible?

In short, it looks as if we can't even *think* at all without making assumptions. *The very process of thought and language is dubious!* Well, if that is the case, if language may itself be part of the general dream or deception, then we can't appeal to the properties of language to get us out of this difficulty, as some philosophers in the twentieth century have tried to do (Wittgenstein, Derrida, etcetera). Language could be part of the general stream of *Maya*—the play of illusion. Hence, there seems to be no end or limit to doubt, no fundamental knowledge to rely on, not even knowledge of language.

In sum: it seems we cannot think or speak in a valid or self-validating way. Communication as such is questionable and voidable. Even communicating that communicating is questionable and voidable is questionable and voidable. Our very thought itself exists in a state of quandary: we are stymied.

There is something important about this radical scepticism that must now be mentioned. It must be stressed at this point because perhaps one is thinking to oneself something like this, 'Well, okay, that's a possibility. We might occasionally doubt all things. But it's all highly *improbable*. I mean, it's much more *probable* that the world existed more than two minutes ago than that it did not.' But actually, this is incorrect. The most staggering and weird thing about radical scepticism is that you cannot even say it is more *probable* that the world existed two minutes ago than that it did not. For *on what basis would you build your probability argument*?

We can only build probability arguments on the basis of a series of past experiences that allow us to calculate probabilities about what the case is or what will happen in the future. But if you cannot establish that the world existed more than two minutes ago you've got no grounds for probability arguments. Probability arguments simply cannot get under way. The most amazing thing about radical scepticism is that we have to conclude, for example, it is just as probable the world did not exist two minutes ago as that it did. Probabilities do not come into it. There is no basis for establishing a probability argument. The most extreme sceptics in the history of Western philosophy seem to have accepted this point; one metaphysical view of reality is just as probable as another.

Hence there is an ancient Greek motto: *ouden mallon*—a motto that sums up the argument by saying 'there is no more likelihood of this being true than that'.[6]

PYRRHONIAN SCEPTICISM

In ancient Greece there were two main schools of scepticism. There was the Academic School, so called because it was based in Plato's Academy. Plato, of course, was not a sceptic. He was a metaphysician who held out the hope of transcendental metaphysical knowledge. He established his Academy in Athens and when he died it was taken over by his nephew, Speusippus (407–339 BC) who was a Platonist. After he died, it was taken over by Xenocrates (396–314 BC), who was also a Platonist. After he died it was eventually taken over by Arcesilaus (316–314 BC), who was influenced by sceptical arguments. He started the tradition of scepticism in the Academy, a tradition of scepticism almost as radical as the one we have been considering. This school thrived for some five or six hundred years.

In addition, there was the school of Pyrrhonian Scepticism, founded by the philosopher Pyrrho of Elis (365–270 BC). Important figures in this tradition are Timon of Phlius (320–230 BC) and Sextus Empiricus, who wrote towards the end of the second century AD. So again this school of scepticism flourished for a long period of some six hundred years. The Academic Sceptics were also called the Probabilists, apparently because they claimed that some things were more probably true than others. The Pyrrhonian Sceptics, on the other hand, denied even probability arguments. They maintained that there was no basis for establishing probability arguments. So it seems they were more radical sceptics than the Academics.

Many scientifically minded sceptics nowadays are limited sceptics. We might say they are more the heirs of the Academic school of Scepticism. For they are happy enough to accept that there is no true or certain knowledge, no complete knowledge, and that not even science supplies such knowledge. However, they still want to say that science supplies a high probability of correctness and a kind of increasing *approximation* to knowledge. They like to put it this way because they are aware scientific theories are liable to revision in time and that, for all we know, future experiments might bring up new results. So they are Probabilists, in that they want to claim that things are 'probably true' in science. The most extreme form of scepticism, however, even denies that such probability claims can be made.

Now let us consider some objections. It might be said that the most radical kind of scepticism, Pyrrhonian Scepticism, is either a) inconsistent, b) totally unhelpful and irrelevant, c) merely a cute academic exercise, or all of the above.

The inconsistency charge would run something like this: 'Well, if radical sceptics doubt and deny everything, don't they also have to doubt and deny reason and thought, and so even sceptical arguments themselves? If so, surely they can't have any arguments at all, not even sceptical ones'.

Pyrrhonian Sceptics react to this argument rather as Nagarjuna did when faced with similar objections to the Madhyamaka philosophy. They reply that the critical dialectician, or the radical sceptic, is merely operating within the assumptions the opponent brings to the table, then using those very assumptions to undermine the opponent's own position. Normally, the opponent, you see, has swallowed certain initial premises and is addicted to believing in something. The radical sceptic's job is to show that those premises and beliefs logically undermine themselves when pushed far enough.

David Hume (1711–1776) in his book, *A Treatise of Human Nature*, also arrived at an extreme scepticism. With regard to reasoning sceptically about reason, he put it this way:

> Reason first appears in possession of the throne, prescribing laws, and imposing maxims, with an absolute sway and authority. Her enemy, therefore, is oblig'd to take shelter under her protection, and by making use of rational arguments to prove the fallaciousness and imbecility of reason, produces, in a manner, a patent under his hand and seal. This patent has at first an authority proportion'd to the present and immediate authority of reason, from which it is deriv'd. But as it is supposed to be contrary to reason, it gradually diminishes the force of that governing power, and its own at the same time; till at last they both vanish away into nothing.[7]

METHOD

The proper procedure in the sceptic approach is to engage in a kind of internal critique where you accept for the time being the first premises or beliefs of the other person's point of view (the value and authority of reason) but then you try and argue in such a way that things fall apart from within. You are quite happy to let your own arguments fall apart as well, so that both 'vanish away into nothing'. Or as we might say: into the voidance, the resulting dumfounded silence or suspense of thought and judgement. The upshot is that rational theory and thought is reduced to its futility. The mind is brought to an impasse—rather as in the case of a Zen koan. The aim is to stymie thought altogether and so reduce it to a critically aware and voided silence, a kind of complete open-mindedness—openness (shunyata).

In short, in this way it is perfectly possible to present radical scepticism as an art of internal critique, and thereby avoid the charge of inconsistency. For the sceptic does not have to assert anything as true: one just plays opponents at their own game.

What now about the charge that 'it is unhelpful, irrelevant, or impractical, to think in this kind of way'? Surely scepticism can't possibly be lived? The radical sceptic would become paralysed and catatonic—or so it may be alleged.

This has been a common objection. One comes across many stories of Pyrrho of Elis, for example, that are very likely apocryphal and designed by opponents. For example, it is said that Pyrrho would not get out of the way of a speeding chariot that was heading towards him because he was not sure that it really existed, and so would have died there and then if it were not for a worldly (relatively un-philosophical) student of his who set aside his scepticism for a moment and pushed Pyrrho out of the way.

However, although sceptics disclaim all knowledge, they need not deny that many things *appear* or *seem* to be real or true or right or best to do. For we can say that such-and-such *seems* to be the case, *seems* to exist, *seems* to be valuable, etcetera, while we also admit that we could easily be wrong. This is similar to what was said in the previous chapter about 'spontaneous personal intuitions'. We have our personal intuitions about various things, but we do not know where these intuitions come from or what their real validity is. Therefore, we do not have to be committed to the idea that they yield the truth about anything.

I suppose Pyrrho of Elis could have said something like this to himself: 'It *seems* to me, for some ultimately unknown reason, that there is a speeding chariot heading my way. And it *seems* to me, for some ultimately unknown reason, that being hit by a speeding chariot is unpleasant and perhaps fatal. And it *seems* to me, for some ultimately unknown reason, that life is worthwhile and preferable at the moment to death. And, finally, it *seems* to me, again for ultimately unknown reasons, I would do well to get out of the way and so I will'.

The radical sceptic does not take what seems or appears to be true or good to actually *be* true or good. So for all that Pyrrho actually *knows*—or anybody else for that matter—it might be better for him to be hit by the chariot and die then and there. Death, for all we know, might be the greatest boon in disguise. It is possible. The sceptic judges and acts, but in a provisional and unattached way, based on intuitions that are understood to be ultimately dubious but that appear as preferable at the time. One 'goes along with them,' as it were, but without any absolute commitment; that is, without being attached to them as reliable sources of the truth. Hence the radical sceptic can maintain a kind of critical non-attachment to the temporal self and the world insofar as he or she is not an addict to the validity of intuitions. In short: he or she is not committed to this or that view of reality. It is this that enables the radical sceptic to void or drop all views of reality in the state of meditative or contemplative openness.

This seems to fit very well with the two-tier approach to truth or reality we find in the Madhyamaka philosophy. There is a relative or mundane level, and there is a more ultimate or absolute level. From the ultimate standpoint of the critical dialectician or the radical sceptic all views of reality are seen to be shunyata: empty or devoid of self-existence or absolute truth. However, at the relative or mundane level we still have an *appearance* of this or that being believable and true. We must learn to operate at both levels and be able to switch between them at any moment. Thus: we can both act in the world on the basis of what 'seems so' to us while we can also contemplate everything in voidance.

Understood this way, radical scepticism is not at all impractical or impossible to live. We still have our personal intuitions, hence we can still act and function in the mundane world of appearances. One does not become paralysed or catatonic. It is just that one is no longer addicted to one's personal intuitions being true, for they might actually be false. Not being addicted—that means one can see through one's construction of reality and let go of thoughts and beliefs to 'suspend judgement' in open-mindedness or openness (*shunyata*).

What now about the third objection, the idea that this is merely an academic exercise that has no practical or beneficial consequence? What did the ancient sceptics have to say about that? Quite contrary to the idea that radical scepticism is impractical or useless, the sceptics said that a daily application of scepticism seemed to them to have very beneficial results, results that *seemed* to them rather practical and important.

For instance, consider what Sextus Empiricus wrote in the *Outlines of Pyrrhonism*. In Book One, Section Twelve, he discusses the goal and practical effect of Pyrrhonian Scepticism. He says that the effects are twofold: first of all, what he calls *ataraxia* in ancient Greek, meaning quietude or serenity of mind.[8] This arises directly out of the contemplative suspension of judgement and argument; that is, being in a state of mind where one suspends theory and thought, voiding and letting go of the self and the world, of things being good or bad, or this or that existing, etcetera. You just suspend the whole picture; the whole set of assumptions, and enter the voided experience of *what is*—that *nothingness* (no-thing-ness). This seems remarkably similar to the shunyata meditation arising from the Madhyamaka philosophy. Sextus says the result seems to be a certain tranquillity of mind: the Buddhist would agree.

Secondly, Sextus says another result is *metriopatheia*, which translates roughly as 'a kind of moderating and tempering effect on the passions,'[9] is a quieting of the whole desiring, feeling, and emotional aspect of existence: a virtue of temperance. He says:

> The Sceptic's goal is *ataraxia*, and that as regards things that are unavoidable, it is having moderate *pathe* (i.e., *metriopatheia*)... for when the Sceptic set out to philosophise... he landed in a controversy between positions of equal strength, and being unable to resolve it, he suspended judgment. But while he was suspending judgment there followed by chance... *ataraxia*.[10]

Through practice this generates a moderating influence on the passions in general:

> For the person who believes that something is by nature good or bad is constantly upset; when he does not possess the things that seem to be good, he thinks he is being tormented by things that are by nature bad, and he chases after the things he supposes to be good; then, when he gets these, he falls into still more torments because of irrational and immoderate exultation, and, fearing any change, he does absolutely everything in order not to lose the things that seem to him good. But the person who takes no position as to what is by nature good or bad neither avoids nor pursues intensely. As a result, he achieves *ataraxia*.[11]

If we are not dogmatically assuming that things are *really* good and essential to have, or *really* bad and essential to avoid, or not assuming that the badness or goodness has some kind of self-existence, some kind of absolute value that is not voidable, then we won't be so desperately intent on the pursuit or avoidance of things. Rather, we can have a much more moderate, playful, and flexible (less rigid and dogmatic) approach. Thus, the radical sceptic enjoys serenity of mind by suspending judgements in moments of contemplation, and because of having critical non-attachment to all judgements that this or that is necessarily or truly good to have or truly desirable, or that this or that is truly bad and necessary to avoid, the person also has a moderate tendency in desires. That is, one becomes a person of temperance (*metriopatheia*), meaning that, with regard to the object of desire, one is able to 'take it or leave it' and still maintain the happy disposition (*eudemonia*).

In other words, the radical sceptic has the capacity to be non-addicted to things, because things only *seem* good or bad, but whether they really *are* good or bad is altogether another matter. Thus he or she undermines the factor of 'ignorant clinging and craving' which, of course, according to Buddhism is *tanha*, the cause of *duhkha* or disquiet in our life. This person maintains a more open mind and heart in approaching life and reality—even loss and death, etcetera. This seems, therefore, to be very akin to the Madhyamaka way of release.

However, this is not to say that the radical sceptic is completely beyond being affected at all. Sextus proceeds:

> We do not suppose, of course, that the Sceptic is wholly untroubled, but we do say that he is troubled only by things unavoidable. For we agree that sometimes he is cold and thirsty and has various feelings like those. But even in such cases, whereas ordinary people are affected by two circumstances—namely, by the *pathe* (feelings) themselves, and not less by its seeming that these conditions are by nature bad—the Sceptic, by eliminating the additional belief that these things are naturally bad, gets off more moderately here as well.[12]

In other words, the Sceptic is only human. As human he or she is bound to feel physical pains and disturbances of various kinds from time to time. But the Sceptic is not bringing to the unavoidable physical pains and disturbances of life the *additional* psychological pain of dogmatically assuming that this or that occurrence is really or inherently bad, or should not have happened, etcetera. One is not *aggravating* the painful situation by adding fixated negative judgements about it. One is letting it be without making assumptions. Hence, one is able to accept it with far greater equanimity, thus *ataraxia*. Thus, overall Sextus says the goal is to cultivate ataraxia in all situations and thereby also develop metriopatheia, a virtue of temperance or non-addiction when it comes to objects of desire and aversion.

Let us recall that Sextus Empiricus was a medical doctor as well as a philosopher. He no doubt had some awareness of the therapeutic potential in this philosophy when applied. Psychotherapists today might take note! And as one might expect from a doctor, Sextus is simply advising us that addiction is unhealthy. In this respect he is just like the Buddha. Both are like 'doctors of the soul' saying: we human beings are *addicts* and that is the reason we suffer so much in this life.

If you want to remedy this, then cut out your addictions. Drop your addictions in void contemplation—that is, let go of everything, the whole world, even the idea of your self as a separate identity in time. Drop even your addiction to the belief anything is real. It might be naught but a fleeting illusion or dream. Therefore, drop time and your addiction to pursuing anything, even truth or enlightenment. Drop everything by seeing that everything is dubious—null and void as such. Why cling to the dubious when it could be quite useless and false? But everything is dubious! So why cling to anything? Why cling even to life in this world when, for all you know, death might be perfect liberation? Anyway, you might already be dead! Drop yourself, drop the past, and drop the future! Then who or what are you? As soon as you try to answer that, drop it too! So then what can you think or say? Nothing! So don't think or say anything then! If you do, also see through it. And likewise, when you speak or act, see that it is just provisional, merely based on what *seems* best to you, but that it could be completely wrong. Therefore, don't pursue or believe anything dogmatically, addictively, or obsessively, as if you knew it really matters, when it might not matter at all. With this awareness, let it go. Even when you act to get something that seems good, let it go, because for all you know, it might actually be bad.

With this, one can live and act in a more ironic and playful way, more lightly—in an *en-lightened* way. *Be not addicted to beliefs and desires!* Such is freedom. In sum: Pyrrhonian Scepticism has been too often and too lightly dismissed by people as being merely a useless academic exercise. In reply we can say:

a) That it can be expressed consistently as a philosophy by

stressing how it uses the method of *internal critique*

b) That it does not lead to total catatonia or paralysis or anything impractical because the sceptic can act on the basis of how things *seem* at the time

c) That it does *seem* to have some practical therapeutic benefit with regard to dealing with life and suffering.

One can also say that it has much in common with the Madhyamaka philosophy of shunyata. So we have an excellent example here of how there can be a meeting of minds from East and West: a similarity in wisdom coming from two completely different and independent traditions and cultures.

At ant rate, so it seems to me at the moment. But whether any of this is true or not—who knows? I might have just sprung into existence complete with my own fantasy world. Maybe Satan is tricking me? Some folk might say so. But what can you do when whatever you do might be another trick?

The trick is to be aware of the trick that being aware of the trick might be the trick of being aware of the trick of a trick of a trick...

3

EXISTENTIALISM AND RE-ENCHANTMENT

Life is nothing until it is lived; but it is yours to make sense of, and
the value of it is nothing else than the sense that you choose.
— Jean-Paul Sartre

Although it may seem contradictory to the spirit of existentialism to sum it up in a few basic systematic principles, since existentialism is generally opposed to the whole idea of neat systems of explanation—whether of life and reality or of existentialism itself—for the sake of our exposition, let's temporarily set this consideration aside and simplify the complex matter somewhat by saying there are seven key themes in existentialism. Let us take these seven themes as guiding threads to facilitate our understanding of this philosophy and say these seven themes represent what seems to be most important to most philosophers usually described as existentialists.

SEVEN KEY THEMES

1 EXISTENCE PRECEDES ESSENCE

If one is looking for a short definition of existentialism, the saying that 'existence precedes essence' would surely be the best candidate.

It is, after all, the motto of existentialism provided by the philosopher and author most commonly identified as an existentialist, namely, Jean-Paul Sartre (1905–1980). He provided this formulation in his influential public lecture, 'Existentialism Is A Humanism,' delivered in Paris in 1946.

In a famous passage there he says that, if we think of any article of manufacture, say, a paperknife, we can see it has been made by an artisan who had a prior conception of it—an idea of it in his head, a kind of blueprint. He paid attention to this idea of it in making the thing to be as it is. The paperknife is made to be a certain something, with a certain form and nature, and it can be said to have a definite purpose or role to play or a certain function in the overall scheme of things.[1]

We can put it that the *essence* of the paperknife is the blueprint behind its production, the idea of its form and nature, its purpose and function in the scheme of things–its *raison d'etre*. We could also say that its *essence precedes its existence*. The idea and meaning of the thing comes first, and then this explains the existence of the thing. Also, in principle, the thing can be exhaustively defined in terms of its essence. If you have a full and complete grasp of something's essence in concepts–its form, nature, meaning, purpose, place and function—then you can define it and understand thoroughly *what it is* and *what it is for*. You will make its existence thereby intellectually intelligible because you will understand the idea behind its production, the reason for its existence, its why and wherefore. There will be a *why* for it, as it were.

Generally speaking, the *essentialist* approach in philosophy is to believe in and seek for the essences of everything, including the human being, and use either reason or religious revelations to attempt to discover what this real essence is for any object. On either approach the view will be taken that there really is an idea 'out there' in some objective sense of how everything ought to be, how it ought to function, what its place is in the overall scheme of things, and what is the goal or purpose or meaning of its existence.

God, for example, could have created everything, rather like a divine artisan, with some prior blueprint or essential idea like this, just as Sartre's artisan creates the paperknife. According to this view everything has a reason to be: nothing exists without a reason or *without a why*. This has been summed up in the *Principle of Sufficient Reason*: that everything has an essential reason and cause for its existence, for why it is what it is, and for why it occurs when and where it does in the scheme of things. Therefore, everything is, in principle at least, intellectually intelligible and can be fully explained—is explicable—if we can just discover and capture the conceptual essence of things in our philosophy and thought, that is, in our *logos* (reasoned account).

Perhaps the most pertinent point for us human beings about this essentialist picture of things is that there is said to be an essence of humanity as well, a human essence, and therefore a preset idea of the reason for our existence, a reason that establishes objectively how we ought to be, how we ought to live, what we ought to be aiming at with our lives, what the meaning of our lives ought to be, what moral values we ought to aspire to, and what we ought to do to find true fulfilment and *our proper place* in the scheme of things.

It is precisely this that is vigorously denied by existentialism, which is thus defined in direct opposition to essentialism and its assumptions. According to existentialism, we cannot start off simply with prior essences—that kind of metaphysical scenario, assumed to be true from the first, to be the absolute or 'the given'. Rather, we first find ourselves here and now in existence, already in the midst of life, present and alive and face-to-face with the mystery of things; the sheer strangeness of the fact that we are here at all, we know not why, or whether there is any sense to it. Only later do we attempt to explain existence to ourselves, define ourselves as this or that type of being, or claim to discover answers to this uncanny endless puzzle. The most basic fact, the first fact, is that we are here now, apparently without a particular rhyme or reason. It is from the heart of this initial mystery of existence that we choose, act and think. We proceed somewhat blindly from there, stabbing in the dark of this mystery.

Existentialism maintains that if we are persistent and honest in our philosophical inquiries we will eventually discover that no con- clusive or definitive answers as to why we are here are simply given in the nature of things. The various so-called rational explanations and answers that metaphysical system-builders have dreamed up down through the ages, and the so-called good reasons they have claimed to provide for them, seem utterly inadequate or even comic and ridiculous (as Kierkegaard would say) when probed and con- sidered closely. Every metaphysical scenario seems simplistic and naïve in the face of the profound, often agonisingly perplexing, fun- damental mystery of life. Against this, all the systematic explanations seem feeble and unconvincing—almost an affront, one might say, to the *abyssal depth* of the strangeness of human life and death and the anguish of the human condition.

So in existentialism what we start from is simply 'the upsurge' into consciousness of our here-and-now existence—existence comes first—not from some supposed essence, or essentialist explanation of existence, or any handed-down truth, for immediate existence here and now is the only sure thing and the rest is always to some degree merely metaphysical speculation and assumption. Essentialism is kind of wandering about in abstract thought over the far-flung reaches of apparently infinite space and time. Whereas to be focused on life in an existentialist way is to be concrete, more concerned with the immanent experiences of life, the messy actualities of here-and- now existence, on personal choice and action in the present moment.

Somewhat like Zen Buddhism, though with different assoc- iations, existentialism values an art of living in the present, that is, with a certain present-moment *intensity* of life and awareness, attuned in a revitalised way to the immediate uncanny mystery of life, its choices and its challenges. One might surmise, then, that the purest form of existentialism would insist on the precedence of not only exi- stence over essence but of *Existence Itself* over essence, and so on the frequent return to Existence Itself from any wandering about in abs- tract thought and theoretical speculations. For if the basic principle of existentialism is that existence precedes essence then we remain true to that principle, and so we are most 'authentic' in our existentialism, one would think, if we come back to that immediate existence, that mysterious starting point, in any present moment.

To sum up: Essentialism claims there is some kind of given objective knowledge. It assumes the validity of some 'revealed' systematic explanation or worldview and it imposes this kind of fixed structure on reality in an attempt, as it were, to capture the movement of life in a conceptual box. This systematic structured view is then taken to be the absolute truth about things to which each of us must conform as rational and moral beings. In addition, such an approach sets up certain values, meanings, goals, objects of desire, aspirations, moral ideals, etcetera, as likewise essential and obligatory. The argument will then go that one will not be able to achieve essential human happiness, wellbeing, salvation, or personal fulfilment, etcetera, until or unless one attains to the prescribed ideals and values decreed by the system to be absolutely essential.

If we go along with this, we will be caught; enthralled and fettered by the system. We will be acting in conformity to the dictates of the social and intellectual traditions, to some supposedly essential view of reality handed down to us and give our lives over to the pursuit of these supposedly essential ideals and values. Our view of reality will be narrowed down and confined to this. The essentialist will say that this is true freedom: to follow reason, to obey and to conform. To the existentialist it looks more like blind gullibility and servitude. Nietzsche, for example, condemns it as a philosophy for mere 'herd animals'; for the sheep, as it were, who refuse to think for themselves, be innovative or take the risk of doing things their own way and defying the norms.

2 THE INDIVIDUAL VERSUS THE SYSTEM

This leads us to the second key theme that seems most important to most existentialists: the idea that the living, breathing, thinking,

choosing, passionate, unique, creative, individual person is more crucial, real, tangible and important philosophically speaking—at least
as the vital starting point for philosophy—than any supposedly preset essentialist system or metaphysical scheme of things.

Danish thinker, Soren Kierkegaard (1813–1855), lived and wrote
in the first half of the nineteenth century, at a time when northern
Europe was dominated by the imposing figure of Georg Wilhelm
Hegel (1770–1831) and his essentialist philosophy. The Hegelians
claimed to have discovered the true objective system of reality, the
goal of history, and our role and place in the general scheme of things.
For the typical Hegelian of the period, the rational system of reality
and history was absolute, was everything, and the living individual
was only a kind of tiny cog in the cosmic machinery—relatively fleeting and insignificant compared to the grand sweeping cosmic plan.

The view was that history marches on relentlessly in its proper
course toward a rationally necessary goal. Everything that happens
has to happen the way it does, so that the whole may unfold precisely
as it should in accordance with its own inherent principles of rational
self-development. Hegelians believed that such a metaphysical system objectively exists: moreover, that they could actually *prove* by
dint of pure reason and logic alone that it *is* the objective truth of
things, the essential truth, that which must be accepted by any rational moral being. Therefore, what the individual should do is
carefully follow the complex logic of the argument, learn about the
absolute truth, learn how the system requires us to live, and then actually live accordingly. In short: conform. Only in this way can we
human beings fulfil the essential meaning and purpose of our existence. The System And Its Historical Development is what is absolute,
true, and important: the individual is only of secondary importance.
After all, the individual often has to be sacrificed for the greater good
and the grand purpose of history.

Kierkegaard never tired of criticising this dominant philosophy of
his day. As a recalcitrant and unique individual, a passionate philosophical rebel, he pitted himself against it. He argued vigorously,

first of all, that it is logically impossible to prove that any such supposed system really exists as a metaphysical fact or reality, or that it is
anything more than a wild fiction in a philosopher's brain. He poked
fun at it as such, writing:

> If Hegel had written the whole of his logic and then said,
> in the preface, that it was merely an experiment in
> thought in which he had even begged the question in
> many places, then he would certainly have been the great-
> est thinker who ever lived. As it is he is merely comic.[2]

He also stressed that the existing individual is supremely important, more important than any system, for it is the existing
individual who must freely choose for himself or herself what to believe in (to believe in reason, to believe in Hegelianism, to believe in
Christianity, etcetera). *Choice comes first*. And existential choices cannot be *forced* upon us by any feat of reason or science or evidence
alone, nor by any religious authority or tradition. To be sure, an outward conformity might be forced on us perhaps, but one must decide
to believe or not to believe within one's own heart of hearts if the
thing is to be authentically *true for you*. As Kierkegaard wrote in his
Journals, 'the thing is to find a truth which is *true for me*...'[3]

The human predicament calls for a free choice from each existing
individual, and it will be a choice *hazarded* in the face of irreducible
objective uncertainty of life. For the truth is not simply given un-
ambiguously in a handbook of philosophy or in any religious scrip-
ture or revelation. Against those who would take the line of least res-
istance, the relatively easy course of blindly conforming to the norms
of society and whatever the dominant belief-system happens to be at
the time, Kierkegaard would say that they pay too high a price for it.
For although they might get some lazy comfort or social acceptance
from it—from not thinking deeply, taking things for granted—they
are in danger of sacrificing the courage, sincerity, vitality, and intensity of passion involved in making a carefully considered personal

choice in the face of objective uncertainty; that is, in choosing creatively and honestly in the face of the acknowledged risk of error involved.

Fortunately though, the saving grace of any metaphysical system, Kierkegaard would say, is that it is not quite possible in the end for most intelligent human beings to take it seriously and conform to it completely. There are always residual doubts and loopholes, and even believers continue to exercise their human freedom to act in so-called 'irrational' ways, in temporary forgetfulness of the system and how they are supposed to act according to it, for example. After all, no one is perfect, and the messy actualities of everyday life frequently tempt and distract us. Most people fail to live their philosophy in everyday life in a genuine way. Even the systematisers themselves fail to live up to their grandiose principles. As Kierkegaard wrote, 'In relation to their systems most systematisers are like a man who builds an enormous castle and lives in a shack close by.'[4]

For Kierkegaard, the idea that the ultimate truth and purpose of reality had already been given in several volumes of Hegel was too much of an absurdity and insult to the passionate, open-ended, and venturesome nature of human life as actually lived and experienced; that is, in the face of our incomplete understanding as we direct ourselves toward an uncertain future. He wrote:

> It is perfectly true, as philosophers say, that life must be understood backwards. But they forget the other proposition, that it must be lived forwards. And if one thinks over that proposition it becomes more and more evident that life can never really be understood in time simply because at no particular moment can I find the necessary resting place from which to understand it—backwards.[5]

He felt that the imposition of an abstract objective order on everything, this imposition of so-called objectivity or objectivism, was rather akin to squeezing human beings into a kind of cage.

Against the supremacy of the system and of objectivity, he became the great philosophical champion of *not having a system* and of the freedom of radical subjectivity: the freedom of the individual to innovate and hazard his or her own unique view of life and reality. It is the freedom, in other words, to decide for oneself *the meaning of one's own life*. Indeed, make it up as you go along—as we all tend to do anyway! And because of this advocacy of free subjectivity (the subjective choice of one's own personal truth in the face of objective uncertainty), a theme that later on became so central to existentialism, Kierkegaard has been called in retrospect 'the father of existentialism'.

That Kierkegaard was a great champion of free subjectivity is widely known, and he has thereby acquired an important place in the history of Western philosophy. What is not so well known is that, at the very same time Kierkegaard was engaging in his personal vendetta against 'essentialist objectivism' in philosophy, a German philosopher by the name of Max Stirner (1806–1856) was doing much the same thing in his own unique way. In 1844, the year that Kierkegaard published his main book, the *Concluding Unscientific Postscript*, Max Stirner published his book, *The Ego and His Own*. In this remarkable, much maligned, and misunderstood text, Stirner also attacks essentialist objectivism in favour of free subjectivity, championing the free and unique individual against all supposed authorities, whether they be those of the church, or tradition, or history, or humanism, or society, or morality, or science, or reason, or any kind of essentialist objectivity. For example, he proclaims:

> How can one assert of modern philosophy or modern times that they have reached freedom, since they have not freed us from the power of objectivity.[6]

As essentialism assumes there is real knowledge of an objective order, it is a mode of objectivism. Existentialism, then, should be the exact opposite, a mode of radical subjectivism. What Stirner is proposing—*total subversion of the power of objectivity*—could well be regarded as perhaps the most radical and pure type of existentialism. It radically empowers free subjectivity against all so-called authorities and thereby against all so-called essential truths, whether of religion or faith or reason or science or even of so-called commonsense. They can all be critically undermined, subverted, deposed, and annulled at the will and whim of free subjectivity. It is not that we would then have no beliefs at all, no thoughts, no discourse, no goals, no desires, etcetera, but that free subjectivity can subvert them all at any time and so one can *absolve* oneself of them.

Thus they would not have dominion or supremacy over us. *A free subjectivity would possess them; they would not possess free subjectivity.* Free subjectivity would be the owner of them, as Stirner puts it, and as owner, would be able to employ and enjoy them in life for various purposes, while also being free to dissolve and consume them or, as Stirner says, return them all to the nothingness from whence they came. Not only that, the owner returns himself, or the idea he has of himself, to nothingness. This he does on the very last page![7]

This is very interesting, for here this radical and pure form of existentialism begins to sound quite like Madhyamaka Buddhism, insofar as in both cases genuine freedom in life is understood in terms of the subjective ability to *violate* and *void* every so-called 'sacred truth' and thereby return everything back to zero—shunyata. *(emptiness)*

3 THE ENCOUNTER WITH NOTHINGNESS

This now brings us to the third great theme in existentialism: the idea that what life and existential honesty require of us is: *an encounter with nothingness.*

This term *nothingness* can be used in different ways by different existentialists, however. For example, Jean-Paul Sartre used the term mainly to refer to human *consciousness*. Human consciousness, as something intangible, free, metastable, fluid, shifting and not at all a fixed and solid being like a stone or a paperknife, cannot be thought of as a *thing* at all, or as a *thing among other things*, fixated in being. So it might reasonably be called a *non-thing*, a *no-thing*—hence a kind of nothingness. Not nothingness, of course, in the sense of something that simply does not exist at all, but rather as something that exists, but not at all in the way that things exist.

Alternatively, Martin Heidegger (1889–1976) sometimes used the term *nothingness* to refer to Being with a capital B—that is, that which is the ground or source of all particular, limited, finite, determinate *beings*, but is not itself a determinate being among beings. As this encompassing totality is not itself a being among beings, a thing among things, it can reasonably be called a *non-thing* or *no-thing*—a kind of Nothingness (perhaps best with a capital N). Again it does not mean something that doesn't exists—for after all, we are here talking about Being with a capital B—but something that doesn't exist in the way beings or things exist, as a particular, differentiable, conceptualised, separate limited entity among or alongside others of the kind.

Alternatively again, Max Stirner speaks of *himself* as a kind of nothingness. That is, one's own immediate existence here-and-now is a rather strange power of creative awareness that eludes all religious or rational definition, any definition at all in concepts, since what one really is cannot be pinned down by mere thoughts and so-called essential truths. On the contrary, this conscious presence exists even prior to one's thoughts and self-determinations as a kind of *indeterminate power of determination*. Put it this way: as the interpreting consciousness, one is not the interpreted object, but the interpreting source. Hence, one has this immediate mode of existence in the present, but not as an interpreted and determinate entity among others.

As free subjectivity is not a *thing*, provisionally it can be called a *nothingness*. Although, as Stirner points out, one is not merely an inert nothingness, but a creative nothingness. For this 'creative nothing' has the power to decide how to appropriate or own the world in interpretations and concepts, as well as how to dissolve and annul it again. To be this creator and dissolver of interpretations of reality is what Stirner means by taking ownership of everything. And he really means everything! For instance, he writes, 'And now I take the world as what it is to me, as mine, as my property.'[8] And again, 'I am the owner of the world of things, and I am owner of the world of mind.'[9] Moreover, as regards others, he says that, 'to me you are only what you are for me—to wit, my object; and because my object, therefore my property.'[10] That is, since everything is for me in accordance with my interpretation of it, everything is my object, hence my property. Thus, one becomes 'the owner' in Stirner's unique sense through a self-empowering philosophical reflection and awareness of oneself as the evaluator and interpreter of everything in one's world.

One might now surmise the following from all this: if in the purest form of nothingness all conceptual systems and determinations of reality have been dissolved and annulled, then there is surely no way left to distinguish *the nothingness that one is as free subjectivity* from *the nothingness of the rest of reality*—or from the general is-ness of what is. Hence, surely one arrives—not exactly at monism (that is, at a metaphysical concept or theory that reality is one) but at an experiential non-dualism (that is, at the suspension of all the conceptual distinctions and discriminations that separate one thing from another). In short, at that point, the ultimate 'encounter with nothingness' would no longer be an encounter as such—which rather implies a distinction, a conceptual and ontological separation between the subject doing the encountering and the object encountered. Rather, there would be the voidance of any separation between subject and object.

That indeed seems to be what Stirner means when he blurs the distinction between himself and his property—every object of awareness and interpretation. For instance, he uses the lines, 'Get the value out of your property!' and 'Get the value out of thyself!' interchangeably.[11] And he writes, 'My power is my property. My power gives me property. My power am I myself, and through it am I my property.'[12] There is no clear distinction between self and property, between self and object of awareness. Moreover, on the very last page of his book, he says that free subjectivity—which he has hitherto called the ego, the self, the owner, free egoism, etcetera—is returned

processing:
past
present
future

to creative nothingness. He says there that, 'the owner himself returns to his creative nothing, of which he is born'.[13] At that point there is only creative nothing, for all ideas and distinctions, both of self and of property, have been consumed.

Interesting, for it implies that when the logic of pure existentialism is pushed far enough—the logic of radically free subjectivity, subjectivity that has relentlessly attacked and subverted the power of objectivity, subjectivity that is nothing but the upsurge of a pure existence preceding essence—then subjectivity itself is also dissolved and annulled. For without any object there can be no subject. That is to say, no distinction remains between the two. If so, we do not have the 'encounter' of a subject with a separate nothingness, but rather we simply have non-dual nothingness: a nothingness where there is no basis for a distinction between subject and object, where the distinction is voided—shunyata.

Therefore, contrary to what is usually said in existentialism, or about existentialism, the ultimate in existentialism, in free subjectivity, is not any kind of so-called *alterity*; that is, any kind of ontological dualism of the subject or ego facing separate others, or up against a world considered as other, as enemy, as brute being-in-itself, as a kind of nauseating or alien or alienated otherness, etcetera. Rather, it is the very dissolution of ontological dualism: this entire sense of otherness, this sense of separation or alienation from others, or from the world, or from an external will or fate. Somewhat paradoxically, free subjectivity, after it has annulled everything else, ends by annulling itself—and along with it, all division and divisiveness. Hence: all hostility, all *enmity* as such. Peace and harmony arise when there are no separate beings to be in disharmony with, when there is no longer the basis, the philosophical grounds, for a hostile attitude of opposition between subject and object, between the subject and 'the other'. In short, when there is no longer any ontological duality.

As we have said previously, the Madhyamaka philosophy of shunyata and the most extreme Pyrrhonian suspension of judgement, also arrive at such an experiential non-dualism through the undermining and subversion of thought and belief. For this would void and suspend the ontological distinctions between the so-called self and the not-self.

To conclude on this theme: in addition to this, the term *nothingness* has also been used in existentialism to refer to the general 'vanity' of our various life projects, goals, meanings, speculations, and even our pursuit of so-called 'real being'. We are, after all, a kind of ephemeral existence, impermanent, always choosing and changing—a *becoming*, then, rather than a fixed or stable *being* as such. Also, we cannot rely on anything for sure: our past might be a dreamlike illusion and we could cease to exist in the very next moment. Also, our life projects may not amount to anything at all, or mean anything: they may well be pointless and pretentious vanities relative to the universe itself or the ultimate truth (whatever that is). Also, as we have seen, our profoundest thoughts and most cherished beliefs about life and reality could merely be tricks, deceptions, false lights, illusions; superficial and worthless as straw.

Our lives could be naught but some airy insubstantial dream, as Shakespeare said, 'such stuff as dreams are made on'. Or, as he also put it, 'Life could be a tale told by idiot, full of sound and fury, signifying nothing'. And, of course, whoever was the author of Ecclesiastes in the Bible may well have been right in saying that 'all is vanity under the sun'. To live in existential honesty, and not humbug ourselves with our self-importance, we must retain awareness of this factor of the potential vanity and voidness of human life and not kid ourselves on that we know what we are doing or what we are talking about. Yes, even me, right here, right now! This book too: perhaps it is much ado about nothing and mere vanity. Could be!

4 EXISTENTIAL AUTHENTICITY

A fourth key theme in existentialism is this emphasis placed on the value of intellectual integrity or existential honesty, often referred to as *existential authenticity*. Existentialists generally say that, if we are living and philosophising as human beings in a genuine or authentic way, then we will be courageous, unique, venturesome, honest, and passionate in our approach to life and its many perplexing issues. We will be constantly returning to, focussing on, and facing squarely up to, all these rather unsettling or challenging doubts and questions, not trying to escape and evade them by immersing ourselves in every-day busyness, practical affairs, social conformism, family life, romantic and sexual pursuits, media entertainments and other such superficial distractions. Likewise, our preferred arts and philosophies will be ones that 'go for the jugular,' so to speak; that is, that home in on these existential issues and revitalise them, not ones that sweep them under the carpet and gloss them over with merely academic int-ellectualism, data-bytes and information, technical proficiency and jargon, essentialist speculations and dogmatism, or endless thoughts and idle debates, including whatever goes on restlessly in one's head.

To live authentically in the existentialist way we must confront the darker and more uncanny aspects of life that we, in our everyday busyness, generally like to ignore, evade or avoid—the factor of death, for example. As death is a part of life, one is being less than honest with oneself if one evades the issue. Moreover, it could even be that evading the issue out of existential anxiety might actually be making it worse: for we tend to reinforce our fears by running away from them or trying to ignore them. They may be suppressed tem-porarily this way, but they continue to fester in the mind. Perhaps, then, it would not only be more honest and courageous to face up squarely to an existential issue such as death, but it might also be the most healthy or empowering course to take in the long run.

The inevitability of personal death is approaching us with every passing moment, with every breath we breathe. And since time seems to fly by, slipping through our fingers, the final moment of death will be upon us all too soon, as if quite suddenly, one imagines, and there will be no time: for the past will have vanished away like snow on the water. Likewise, in authenticity, we must address squarely the con-tingent nature of human life—that random accidents happen at any moment, that everything slips and changes, that people and things get broken and lost, that nothing can be relied upon, that nothing can be held on to securely, that everything is strange and uncertain, etcetera. And again, perhaps the ultimate to be aware of in existential authenticity is this uncanny factor of nothingness—that one's very life is a kind of nothing. Even if this awareness does generate in us a powerful initial sense of deep unease, let us look to our nothingness: perhaps it is the very lifeblood of philosophy. For through philosophy human beings attempt to give some meaning to that nothing, to make nothingness itself creative, to make something interesting and perhaps re-enchanting out of it.

So, no more procrastination! Let's face it, there is only you and your nothing. That is all you've got to work with.

5 ANGST: EXISTENTIAL ANXIETY

This brings us to the fifth key theme in existentialism: the emphasis given by most existentialists to the mood of *angst* in life. This word is often left untranslated, but when it is translated it is usually rendered as existential anxiety, or existential dread, or anguish or perhaps ontological insecurity. This type of anxiety is carefully distinguished from ordinary anxiety: a fear directed toward some specific thing, such as the fear of an intruder, or a fear of spiders, etcetera. Existential anxiety is not directed toward a specific thing as such. Rather, it is directed toward the aforementioned general existential themes—the basic features of the human condition—and ultimately toward the factor of nothingness. Just as most people tend to want to evade and avoid thinking about or encountering or experiencing death, so most people tend to want to evade and avoid thinking about or encountering or experiencing nothingness, for both quicken the sense of angst.

Some existentialists, notably Sartre, insist that anguish, existential anxiety, dread, is a kind of final or supreme emotion in human life, the most existentially authentic emotion we can experience and the one that best reveals the basic features of our human condition. However, not all existentialists would agree with this. While they all recognise that some anxiety or dread is involved in facing up to the human condition and undermining our comforting illusions, not all of them would say that angst is the final or supreme emotion. Some would say it is only an initial or transitional emotional phase we go through in our existential development, and that if we face up to the anxiety robustly, and live with it for a time, we can eventually grow beyond it. We may begin to discover that a much more positive emotional experience can develop from the process of undermining everything and letting it go, even getting right down to zero, to nothingness. The authentic encounter with nothingness can eventually be experienced as a kind of liberation, as emancipation, rather than as a source of relentless uncanny dread.

This emancipation can be an empowerment: something joyful and affirmative in effect. This at least is the kind of line taken by Stirner and Nietzsche. Nietzsche, for example, sees the encounter with nothingness and nihilism as being self-liberating because it frees us to choose to take an unconditionally positive and courageous perspective: to adopt what he calls the Yes-saying attitude of the free spirit. One subverts the *power of objectivity* to be *free for* this kind of groundless and unconditional affirmation of the total process of life.

We might also note that, although Martin Heidegger tended to emphasise the dark and uncanny aspect of angst or dread in his early writings—especially in so far as angst is occasioned by thoughts of death—in his later writings he moved away from this. The angst or dread becomes more akin to a feeling of awe. Still later in his writings, he indicates that this awe is by no means incompatible with *serenity*.[14] It rather appears as if Heidegger may have gone through a process of personal existential development regarding this matter.

No doubt the encounter with nothingness initially generates some dread—for, after all, one does have to learn to abandon everything to which one has been clinging for security—but it can later change from dread to awe to serenity as one becomes more familiar with the existential situation and more 'acclimatised' to it, as it were. In Buddhism, somewhat similarly, although dwelling in meditative nothingness may feel so upsetting at first that one tends to avoid doing the practice, or one distracts oneself from it even while doing it, with prolonged practice one eventually finds it can be indeed be calming, beneficial, liberating, empowering, enlightening, and conducive to serenity and life affirmation.

6 FREEDOM AND AFFIRMATION

This brings us to the sixth key theme in existentialism: the importance placed on human freedom and creative affirmation. For example, Sartre wrote that the essential truth of the existence of God and objective values is not a given, and consequently he accepted Dostoevsky's proposition that, if this is the case, then 'all is permitted'. Indeed, Sartre sees this as the genuine starting point for existentialism.[15] Nothing is given; therefore we ourselves are the sole creators of value. One realises, 'I am the being by whom values exist'. One is subjectively free then to create and to realise one's own values and perspectives on life since none are given as objectively true or essential. One is free, in other words, to create value in and from one's creative nothingness, and thereby, as Stirner says, 'Get the value out of thyself!'[16]

Hence, it seems, we are emancipated in virtue of our creative nothingness to be as positive and unconditionally affirmative about the whole of life as we like, as we please, at our own groundless will and whim. Stirner and Nietzsche certainly avail themselves of this kind of freedom and creativity. They reveal how a freewheeling free spirit, free subjectivity, can create and determine its own value and the value of the totality of life as supremely positive. Thus one would become a kind of Nietzschean Yes-sayer of life, or one would generate for oneself what Stirner calls 'the self-enjoyment of life'.[17]

In this way our existential freedom and creativity can be exercised for an unconditional affirmation of the whole of existence

—beyond objectivism, and beyond the duality of the subjective and objective. Beyond the initial angst of the so-called 'encounter with nothingness' there is the possibility of a very positive, non-dualistic, and holistic affirmation of what is. In short: an absolute life affirmation. Indeed, even Sartre, despite his own gloomy tendencies, declared in 'Existentialism Is A Humanism' that:

> Life is nothing until it is lived; but it is yours to make sense of, and the value of it is nothing else than the sense that you choose.[18]

Well now, if that is so, then there is really nothing at all requiring us to be pessimistic, gloomy, or angst-ridden, or be the kind of perennially anguished existentialist that Sartre represented and championed. For it is entirely up to us as free existentialists to set the value of things for ourselves, and we can choose to set this value as high as we like, as high as possible—as supreme, as perfect, as ideal. Like Max Stirner we can declare that there is no separation between the real and the ideal,[19] and approve his declaration that, 'We are perfect altogether.'[20] Indeed, why not? For it is up to us to get the value out of our self and our property—every object of awareness; all and everything. We can declare it 'perfect altogether' and so consume it in self-enjoyment.

Quite contrary to what that gloomy Frenchman and other gloomy existentialists have said in the past, there is actually nothing at all in existentialism compelling us to say angst, anguish, having a pessimistic perspective on life or viewing life as tragic is really more 'authentic,' in life or in existentialism, than having a free-spirited, self-enjoying, holistically affirmative view of life. All that talk of 'the tragic sense of life', whew! There is nothing stopping us raising high the value of every single aspect and moment of life, every detail of reality, and declaring it entirely right and perfect, even ideal, even as it is, right here, right now. One simply exercises one's freedom and creativity, as one pleases. One dissolves the idea too, as one pleases.

As for Sartre, it must follow from his own stated principles in 'Existentialism Is A Humanism,' that if he saw life as gloomy and anguishing, it was only because he chose to give his life this kind of rather tragic or pessimistic meaning and estimation. For after all, there is no 'power of objectivity' determining that he (or we) *must* see it that way. Rather, as a free existential subjectivity he might just as soon have chosen to see it in a completely different light, by giving it the meaning and value of a challenging but rewarding adventure, for instance. Let us not be fooled by *his* choice; existentialism *can* be a positive and playful philosophy.

With or without little goatees, beware of existentialists wearing black, not to mention postmodern critical theorists, deconstructionists and the like! If they say that to be authentic and critical about society, about the state of the world, about 'the slaughter bench of human history,' etcetara, one must be tragic and dark, then we can simply pull the rug out from under their feet by being more sceptical than they are; that is, by critically undermining the very idea of the tragic and the absurd or their sense of moral despair over the human condition. Judgemental self-righteous morality, after all, is but just one more essentialist ideology.

Moreover, as Nietzsche might say, this modern/postmodern pessimism, this decadent world-weariness and cynicism, this pity and misery over suffering in this world, this late-Western culture, smells suspiciously like residual Christian anti-world moralism, albeit one shorn of the Christian God. People will say, of course, that the pains of life are simply bad; end of story. But no, it's not that simple. For example, if a dentist is drilling a tooth the experience may well be painful, but we don't think it is bad if it serves a good purpose: indeed, we choose it if have to and we bear it with fortitude. The badness of pain depends on the overall context. Now, if there are no given essentialist metaphysical truths, then it is not an essential truth that the pains of life are bad, for it all depends on the overall metaphysical context in which the pains of life occur. You don't know what that is and neither do I. So there is no need to jump to a negative conclusion about it. Indeed, for all we know, the pains of life serve a perfectly good metaphysical purpose in the whole. We can choose to assume so until or unless someone can prove otherwise. Hence we can affirm life as it is in this world.

7 PLAYFUL ENGAGEMENT WITH LIFE

This brings us to the seventh and final theme. Once we have fully realised our creative existential freedom we can then exercise it for some purpose in the world that seems good to us, for some preferred commitment or engagement with life and action.

In his unnecessarily negative way, Sartre put it that, 'man is condemned to be free'.[21] But this so-called 'condemnation' simply means that we cannot avoid making choices in life and so committing ourselves to engage in this or that course of action, at least temporarily, since even to choose not to choose is itself a choice and commitment. Also, if existentially honest, we realise, of course, that in choosing we are taking a big risk—the risk of error, of choosing wrongly and committing ourselves to something that may prove false, an idle vanity, etcetera. The factor of risk is unavoidable, because we cannot avoid choosing and because we can never know what the real truth of life is. The course of action or way of life we choose is only a kind of wager or gaming—and we may appropriately call it a fallible commitment.

As discussed previously, we choose and act in accordance with our personal intuitions about what seems best to us at the time. These intuitions are not well founded at all. We don't even know for sure where they come from. Yet one must stake one's life on something and, whatever it is—for example, Buddhism—we could be completely wrong. But so what? It may still seem more appealing or preferable to us compared to the alternatives on offer. So we go with it. We engage. And yet, we are also aware of the potential vanity, the voidness, the dubiousness, the possibility of error, etcetera. Therefore, we are *engaged*, and yet, by way of the awareness of vanity and voidance, we are also in a sense *disengaged*. Thus, we are in a state of *engaged disengagement*.

This may sound rather odd at first. Engaged disengagement? But actually this can be offered as an excellent description of what it means to be in a *state of play*. For when playing—as in a game or in the theatre—we are in a sense engaged wholeheartedly in the action, and yet, because it is only a game, a bit of theatre, an ultimately non-serious enterprise, a dubious and temporary construction of reality or field of play, we are inwardly, deep down and ultimately, also disengaged. This is to say, one can play with zest and enthusiasm for one's goals in the world but one can and one does also void this temporary construction of reality, this provisional field of play. One can return it and oneself to nothingness at any moment. Therefore, this way of play in life, understood as an engaged disengagement, will be how we pursue our fallible commitments. *Play will be our mode of action.* For instance, it will be how we approach writing a book, particularly a book that talks a lot about play.

POSITIVE EXISTENTIALISM, SHUNYATA MEDITATION AND RE-ENCHANTMENT

Given all this, the idea of synthesising and harmonising existentialism with Madhyamaka Buddhism should not seem so unlikely or surprising by now. For the main themes of the kind of positive existentialism depicted here have a recognisable similarity to central themes in the Madhyamaka schools of Buddhism—perhaps most notably, to Zen. In short, we end up with a kind of Zen Existentialism.

For example, the theme that existence precedes essence focuses us on the value and importance of living in the present moment of life, and this theme also occurs in Zen Buddhism. The rejection of all metaphysical and intellectual systems for describing and explaining reality is also a feature of the shunyata schools of Buddhism, such as Zen. The experience of nothingness is pivotal in both as well, as is the idea that we human beings tend to try and avoid this encounter, rather dishonestly or in an inauthentic way, by clinging to our comforting illusions and distractions. Also present in both is the theme that, if we do frequently dwell in nothingness (called *mu* in Zen) and embrace the initial anxiety this may occasion, we can come through the process to experience nothingness in a very positive way and reach a new standpoint of peace and joy in life.

Let me now approach the completion of this topic by quoting from one important commentator on Buddhism who has also recognised a similarity between Buddhism and existentialism, namely, the Buddhist scholar, Edward Conze. In his book, *Buddhism: Its Evolution and Development*, he says:

> The discoveries which psychologists and philosophers have made in recent years about the central importance of anxiety at the very core of our being have quite a Buddhist ring about them. According to the views elaborated by Scheler, Freud, Heidegger and Jaspers, there is in the core of our being a basic anxiety, a little empty hole from which all other forms of anxiety and unease draw their strength ... It may come upon you when you have been asleep, withdrawn from the world; you wake up in the middle of the night and feel a kind of astonishment at being there, which then gives way to fear and horror at the mere fact of being there. It is then that you catch yourself by yourself, just for a moment, against the background of a kind of nothingness all around you, and with a gnawing sense of your own powerlessness, your utter helplessness in the face of the fact that you are there at all. Usually we avoid this experience as much as we can, because it is so shattering and painful. Usually I am very careful not to have myself by myself, but the I plus all sorts of other experiences. People who are busy all the time, who must always think of something, who must always be doing something, are incessantly running away from this exper-

ience of the basic and original anxiety. What we usually do is to lean and rely on something else than this empty centre of ourselves. The Buddhist contention is that we will never be at ease before we have overcome this basic anxiety, and that we can do that only by relying on nothing at all.[22]

In both Buddhism and existentialism, importance is placed on this idea of properly experiencing and acclimatising to nothingness, learning how to enjoy life from this standpoint, relying only on this creative nothingness that we are. In Zen or Buddhist terms, this is to live in and from an awareness of shunyata. As was said in chapter one, shunyata should not be understood in a mystical sense. The awareness of shunyata is not the same as what is usually called a mystical experience. Rather, as Frederick Streng says in his book, *Emptiness, A Study In Religious Meaning*:

> The awareness of 'emptiness' is not a blank loss of consciousness, an inanimate empty space; rather it is the cognition of daily life without the attachment to it. It is an awareness of distinct entities, of the self, of 'good' and 'bad,' and other practical determinations; but it is aware of these as empty structures. Wisdom is not to be equated with mystical ecstasy; it is rather the joy of freedom in everyday existence.[23]

According to this kind of interpretation, the aim in Madhyamaka Buddhism is not some sort of escape from, or mystical transcendence of, everyday experience with its usual content—awareness of the self, of the distinction between self and not-self, of time and space and the many things of everyday experience. Rather, the aim is to have the insight to be able to void these structures; the so-called 'objective order,' or 'the power of objectivity'. To have this shunyata insight into things here-and-now is to contemplate or meditate on existence unhindered by beliefs, desires, and delusions. As the Tibetan Lama, Chogyam Trungpa Rinpoche says in his book, *Cutting Through Spiritual Materialism*:

> Cutting through our conceptualised versions of the world with the sword of 'prajna' (insight) we discover shunyata—nothingness, emptiness... [24]

The sword of insight is sharp, and it can be wielded at any moment to cut straight through our web of thoughts and assumptions. To experience and appreciate this we just have to suddenly open the mind and heart to the immediate aesthetic quality of Existence Itself. And to open the mind and heart to the immediate aesthetic quality of Existence Itself we have to learn how to subvert everything and annul it—annul our dualistic prejudices against life as it is, in other words. If we do so, we may then come to the rather existentialist realisation that Shakespeare expresses in the play, *Hamlet* (where he was probably borrowing from the Pyrrhonian Sceptics), where he says, 'There is nothing either good or bad but thinking makes it so'.[25]

Now, if Sartre had only realised this he would have seen that life is only gloomy or tragic or 'a useless passion,' etcetera, if one *thinks* it is. Albert Camus (1913–1960) might have realised that life is only absurd or meaningless if one *thinks* it is. Well, if these existentialists want to think that way, that's up to them. But really, as existentialists, they shouldn't be going around presenting it as if that kind of personal view is some kind of *essential* truth, and oh dear, saying we will not be authentic unless we see it this way too and are appropriately angst-ridden about it. My goodness, how *essentialist* is that!

We begin to see that the judgement of life is free and arbitrary. Realising this, we find in creative nothingness our freedom to think and create the whole of reality as good, as perfect, as ideal—if we like it so, if it pleases us—and so adopt this view as our preferred working hypothesis, or existential project, or fallible commitment or mode of play, for whatever benefit it may bring. We may choose it this way as long as we like, until or unless someone can prove that we are essentially wrong in that view. And when will they be able to do this? Never it seems! At any rate, not in this life in this world.

Existentialism has the potential to supply this radical realisation that there is actually nothing at all preventing us from taking a maximally positive view, an optimum view, of ourselves and of reality as a whole, since there are no fixed and essential, objectively true, conceptual systems of reality that we are compelled to accept. We have subverted and voided that old essentialism, and left it behind us, that old power of objectivity and truth. Therefore, we are subjectively free to project a new and very positive perspective on reality. We can become, rather like Nietzsche, a Yes-sayer of reality and of life in this world just as it is, or like Max Stirner we can engage in a practice of the free self-enjoyment of life. That is, we can prefer to adopt these life-affirmative views since no counter-view can ever be proved or established to be true or essential.

In sum, we can choose an optimally positive perspective as our preferred mode of play or fallible commitment until or unless someone can prove it is wrong, which, it seems, they can never do, given radical scepticism and shunyata.

In accordance with Sartre's saying 'life is nothing until it is lived and the sense and value it has will be the sense and value we choose for it,' despite him, we choose to give it a very positive sense and value. We engage in a playful way, in an engaged disengagement, with a holistic affirmation of life, just so. Hence, via this positive version of existentialism we can develop a maximally affirmative kind of personal 'cognitive behaviour therapy,' as it might be called—although it is far more philosophically radical and profound than what usually goes by the name of cognitive behaviour therapy.[26]

However, to get the full and best effect of this personal cognitive behaviour therapy, it is recommended that we also frequently suspend and void everything in meditative nothingness, and dwell in this voidance, in shunyata. For gradually, with this kind of practice, it is no longer simply the same old self with its old conditioned judgements that is present and active. Rather, in contemplation, one suspends this old self and its judgements. One dwells quietly in the still purity of Existence Itself—'sitting quietly, doing nothing,' as Zen says.[27] In this non-dualistic contemplative state, the mind and heart become more open and receptive to the non-dual aesthetic quality of Existence Itself, and one begins to experience something of its free beauty, warmth, peace, harmony, goodness, and wellness—the sense that Existence Itself is not hung-up, that oneself is not hung-up. Contemplative experience of shunyata begins to work in and through the mind and heart while one is being basically passive, voided, letting things be, letting things go.

It is not a matter of jumping in all the time with a free existential choice to affirm that reality is holistically good. Rather, by being aesthetically contemplative, Existence Itself is given some time and chance to reveal something of its goodness and beauty more experientially, naturally, or spontaneously, so that the feeling of wellbeing wells up more from the depths of the mind. One does not try to force this experience, of course, for it cannot be forced. To experience it, the best thing the self can do is to get itself out of the way, to void itself and suspend its judgements in the state of non-dual nothingness. If this is done, and one dwells frequently in this contemplative state, then may occur what Krishnamurti refers to as the benediction of Being—a gathering sense of the peace, wonder, beauty, and the grace of Being. Repeated experience of this benediction begins to transform the self, the mind and heart, in subtle ways, moderating its old conditioning, altering its feelings and intuitions in a more positive and benevolent direction. This has rather a healing and tempering effect on the passions—much as Pyrrhonian Sceptics also said when they spoke of their experience of ataraxia and metriopatheia, their serenity and temperance.

In other words, what is 'skilful' in this overall path, is not just a) free subjectivity holistically affirming the totality of life as it is, and not just b) voiding all thought and sitting passively in meditative nothingness or the contemplation of the aesthetic quality of non-dual Existence Itself. Rather, it is an ongoing interplay between both practices: a double game, so to speak. Therefore, when it comes to thinking and philosophising about life using language, words, concepts, etcetera, one can refer everything ultimately to a preferred holistic and poetic vision of the totality of life as interconnected, unified, and good through and through. When it comes to relaxing from all this wordy philosophising, one simply voids it again in meditative nothingness and aesthetic contemplation. With daily practice, we learn to switch from one to the other at any time, or one can spend some prolonged time in one practice or the other, as one pleases. One can become a master of communication and a master of silence both.

It is the subtle and gradual effect of the meditation practice working hand-in-hand with the existential freedom to affirm everything as a whole that re-enchants life.

Now, all a so-called doctor can do—whether a Buddha or merely a doctor of philosophy—is recommend such a practice to people. It is entirely up to them, in their existential freedom, to choose whether they want to adopt and apply it or not. The fact is, many people, like Sartre or Camus etcetera, seem to get their kicks from being pessimistic, absurdist, tragic, romantic, addicted or darkly melodramatic about their life. Or perhaps it is just that they are used to this, so used to it that it feels to them like it constitutes their very sense of self-identity. And so, for this reason, they are loathe to give it up—even if they do also say, from time to time, that they would like a change, or they would like to be happier in life. This too may be just part of their pattern, after all. Well, if people want to be tragic, or drama queens, or whatever, that is fine. That is their affair. One need only object if they try to argue that there is something more authentic or essentially human about it as if this was the truth.

Perhaps the free aesthetic re-enchantment of life is not everyone's cup of tea. So be it. They don't even have to drink tea. Nevertheless, moving further into the contemplative aspect of the experience of re-enchantment will be the main subject of the next two chapters.

4

RESPLENDENT BEING AND POETIC PLAY

The rose is without why.
– Angelus Silesius

MARTIN HEIDEGGER WAS a German philosopher, counted among the main exponents of twentieth century existentialism. He was an original thinker, critical of modern technological society and its values, and much concerned to help initiate a new beginning, a new dawn, in the history of Western philosophy and culture. He was born and raised a Catholic and showed a strong interest in religion in his youth. This led him to study the late-medieval German mystics, especially the writings of the Christian mystic, Meister Eckhart (1260–1327). Many scholars have noted an affinity between Heidegger's later philosophy and the central themes in Meister Eckhart. Certainly they seem to have some themes in common, and one will be mentioned at the end. However, the mature Heidegger disavowed Christianity as such, and while his approach to Being is reminiscent of Christian Mysticism, it seems, in the last analysis, to be neither Christianity nor mysticism.

His approach is also in some ways reminiscent of Zen, as we will see. We might note here that the very influential Zen scholar D. T.

Suzuki wrote a book entitled, *Mysticism: Christian and Buddhist*, in which he argued that Zen Buddhism and Meister Eckhart are saying some very similar things. If they are very similar and Eckhart is also similar to the later Heidegger, then we can surmise that Zen (or Madhyamaka Buddhism in general) and the later Heidegger is similar too. Similar, of course, does not mean the same. However, that there are some significant affinities between these three has been argued in detail (John D. Caputo's admirable book, *The Mystical Element In Heidegger's Thought*, for example).

Heidegger's main early work is *Being And Time*, published in 1927. In this book the existential philosopher was mainly concern to raise the question: What does it mean to live as a human being with our distinctive mode of consciousness of existence? And also, what does it mean to live authentically in the human mode of being?

This question lies behind but is largely glossed over and obscured by our ordinary everyday life-concerns and consciousness. It is not addressed properly by the sciences and technological thinking either. Indeed, both our 'everydayness' and our 'scientific-technological thinking' tend to distract us from the deeper issues of what it means to live resolutely, courageously, and authentically as a human being. Heidegger, like other existentialists, is concerned to provoke and challenge us to think more honestly and profoundly about the vagaries and strangeness of our human life itself, including its darker and more uncanny aspects—especially the fact of our own inevitable personal death and what that means for us in our lives now.

One of the main pieces of advice he gives in this early work is that we live most authentically and resolutely if we *live-toward-death*; that is, in the full light of this awareness of death and even *directing* ourselves toward death.[1] This living-toward-death will galvanise us, as it were, to a) focus more sharply on the deeper matters of ultimate concern in life rather than waste our time on social entertainments and trivialities, b) fully appreciate and embrace our existence here and now to face our life choices and challenges more robustly, and c) spur us on to live more resolutely, intensely and passionately to make the most of our unique individuality and creative potential while we can.

However, we won't be dealing here with the early work. In the 1930s and 40s Heidegger's thought went through a period of transition that some scholars have called his 'turning around'. This in turn was influenced by his flirtation with and then disillusionment with, the German Nazi Party, and his appreciation of, and studies on, Nietzsche's philosophy of the will-to-power; which he sought to learn from and then get beyond.[2] The result of these two encounters, and the disillusionments to which they led, was that Heidegger turned around, as it were, from focusing on the human view of things—of resolute willpower, authentic thought and courageous action and so on—toward a focus on Being itself. In other words, the main concern of his later philosophy is not so much what the existing individual can authentically will, think, do or achieve by exercising his or her own existential freedom of choice in the face of inevitable death, but somewhat to the contrary, on how we can get ourselves, our egos, our human intellect and willpower out of the way, so that Being can come to the fore and reveal itself in a more authentic, unconcealed manner. It is this later kind of approach that we will consider in this chapter.

ALIENATION FROM BEING

A good point of departure is to note that Heidegger's philosophy arises out of a deep concern that our entire Western culture is now spiritually, morally, and intellectually bankrupt. We have reached a point, he feels, where we have lost our bearings, lost our sense of rootedness and belonging.[3] We no longer feel 'at home' in life, as if we have somehow gone adrift and been cut off from our vital source, from nature, and from existence all around us. What most of us tend to feel most of the time is a sense of individual isolation, separation, and estrangement that tends to generate our modern existential anxiety and unease, a sense that we are *alienated*—from ourselves, from one another, from nature, from the wellsprings of life.

He may have been influenced in his thinking here by Nietzsche.

For Nietzsche had also spoken of how 'God is dead' for modern culture and of how we seem to have entered a period of nihilism and world-weariness, a period of gloom and despair. There is a prevailing sense of the absurdity or meaninglessness of life, a sense of the lack of deep and abiding values. However, the later Heidegger departs from Nietzsche in arguing that the main source of the problem lies in the human will-to-power itself—that human-centeredness that seeks to manipulate Being for its own relatively shallow, repetitive, inauthentic, pragmatic, controlling and egocentric ends.

One expression of this is that we are usually caught up and enthralled in our *everydayness*, as he calls it, what with all the exaggerated importance we give to our busyness and routines, to our everyday anxieties and our *human, all-too-human* niggling worries and strategic objectives. Another expression of it is the way our culture in general has become dominated by the ethics of consumerism and economic rationalism. Another expression of it is the way we have succumbed to the seductions of technology, the mass media, social entertainments, and the scientific, calculative, and manipulative way of viewing nature and life—seeing nature as something to be possessed and controlled for our human-centred or egocentric purposes.

A further, and more fundamental, expression of it—so fundamental it might easily be overlooked—is the way the human intellect and willpower seeks to *grasp* at Being by way of imposing conceptualisations of reality. This has occurred, Heidegger thinks, throughout virtually the whole of the Western epoch of 'metaphysical thinking about Being,' or what Heidegger calls 'representational thinking'. He is in effect calling us to get beyond that whole tradition, to go beyond the *metaphysics* of Being to a more authentic opening and quiet *harkening* to Being.[4]

Representational thinking deals rather abstractly and obsessively with a plurality of things, beings, or entities, as represented in and by our conceptual systems. That is, this thinking divides Being up into a plurality of discrete individual beings or entities for study, and then all our energy and thought is spent on, for example, classifying, labelling, analysing, manipulating, comparing, possessing, controlling, explaining, etcetera, these particular conceptualised beings. We deal all the time with 'beings', particular things, as separated objects. All this thought and effort spent on beings tends to distract us from dwelling on that which is the ground of all beings; that is, on Being Itself, Being with a capital B, the ground and source from which all beings have their being, or emerge and stand forth. It is because we are largely cut off and estranged from this awareness of Being, because we obscure the awareness of Being, because we distract our-selves from it with our ordinary everydayness, with our pragmatic and scientific thinking and our metaphysical systems, that we feel we lack a sense of belonging in and to Being. We lack a sense of profound meaning and value in life—or the *Quality of life*, one might prefer to put it (see Robert Pirsig, *Zen and the Art of Motorcycle Maintenance*, for this idea of Quality).

In sum, we are in a state of alienation from Being, or in a state of *fallenness*, as Heidegger would say. Not a fall from Eden or God as such, but a 'fall from the grace or benediction of Being,' to use Krish-namurti's phrase. We have fallen into a kind of everyday false con-sciousness, living in a kind of enervating fog of habitual thoughts through which we cannot see or experience the grace, wonder, beauty, meaning or value of Being. Being is there all right, but we are simply not open enough to it. One's mind is too dispersed for this; we need be more recollected. Our thoughts wander, our consciousness is too cloudy. Somehow there needs to be a 'clearing' for this experience of Being to occur; to *let* it happen, to *let* Being be, to *let* Being speak.

Heidegger often uses the word *Being*, and sometimes the word *Nothingness* and seems to sometimes use them interchangeably.[5] Why is this? Well, he is very much concerned to distinguish between be-ings—particular beings in the world—and Being Itself, the ground of all beings from which they emerge and stand forth and to which they belong. As *existing*, of course we all have Being: we are all grounded in Being. But this Being, as the source of all existences, or all things, is not itself a *thing*. It is not a thing among things, a separate being

Spiritual

among other separate beings. It is not a particular entity that we encounter in everyday affairs and thoughts. It is, rather, the ground and source of everything as such. Hence, it is not a thing but a kind of non-thing, a no-thing—hence a kind of Nothingness. It is not a No-thing in the sense of something that doesn't exist at all, but in the sense of something that exists, but not in the way that beings exist. This Nothing is reality or existence as a whole, but not any particular entity. He often also uses the phrase 'the abyss of Being' to refer to it.[6] Being is like an abyss, a groundless ground of beings, that cannot be explained, determined, grasped or captured in any representational thinking; any essentialist conceptual system or any metaphysics.[7]

HEID
X
TILLICH

We can't intellectually explain or account for this groundless ground, this abyss of Being, or grasp it in concepts. Strictly speaking, we cannot even *name* it. That is perhaps why he sometimes uses the term Being, and sometimes the term Nothingness, or sometimes uses the term Being, but with a cross through it. Neat trick! This is apparently to indicate that the word is inadequate, that it can be spoken, but that what is spoken must also be cancelled and annulled in silence and stillness. For there is always the danger that the word, even the word of Being, will get in the way of the open experiencing of Being, as it is, beyond words and concepts. We must not confuse whatever *word* we use for it with Being Itself. Moreover, we must not get carried away with our words and thoughts, not even with a theory of Being—not even with a theory of Being that is all about creating a clearing for the experiencing of Being—since this restless parade of words and concepts and theories is what leads us back to the cloudy consciousness that tends to obscure Being.

We can't wilfully *think* Being and hope to get an access to it that way. But we can quietly open ourselves to experiencing Being more directly, fully, intensely, deeply, and authentically, in a clearing in which we cease trying to speak (think, etcetera) Being, but rather let Being speak us, or speak for itself, so to speak.

We can't operate from the human side to manipulate Being, or to create for ourselves, at our will and whim, the fullness or the richness of the genuine experience of Being. For this is not in the direct control of our human willpower. So it is precisely *not* a function of that old familiar idea of the will-to-power that Nietzsche proclaimed and lauded so much—that the Nazi Party later took up and distorted for its own alienated purposes. All we can hope to do is remove the blinkers, the hindrances and the blocks that stop us from being sympathtically receptive to the experience of Being and from being at one with Being. What we must do, in effect, is redeem our fallenness—our everyday alienation from Being—by clearing away the foggy false consciousness generated and maintained by busyness and relatively petty concerns, handed-down metaphysical presuppositions and human will-to-power. Getting beyond that, we can return to our vocation, as it were, to harken to Being. In other words, let us have a more profound and more authentic encounter with Nothingness; now understood as the open experiencing of Being. And only by so doing will Being Itself (not ourselves, as such, with our human willpower) overcome the plight, malaise, existential alienation, angst or disease that afflicts us and our entire culture in this epoch.

OVERCOMING PHILOSOPHY

Heidegger would like to be able to proclaim that the rule of traditional philosophy as metaphysics, or traditional intellectualism, the rule of discursive reason and theory—even in the form of critical theory or critique or deconstruction—is finally at its *end* today.[8] That is why we hear a lot of talk these days about 'the end of philosophy,' etcetera. For, it seems, the old noble enterprise has failed. It has failed to provide us with secure and abiding truths or ethics, and it has failed to provide us with individual or social wellbeing, belongingness, peace of mind or happiness. The whole tradition from Plato to Nietzsche has been wrongly orientated from the start, he says. For it has been orientated toward beings in the *forgetfulness* of Being. In other words, it has been overly concerned with intellectualising about life and reality, grasping it in some grand theory or system—or else criticising theories from the standpoint of some other theory—rather than with a real opening to the Being experience in its own kind of 'truth'. Therefore, he speaks of the need of our times as a need to bring this tradition of Western philosophy to an end, to 'overcome philosophy' in this way.[9]

However, it shouldn't be thought that this overcoming of philosophy is a mere rejection of it from the outside, or a mere ignoring of it—as something hopelessly impractical compared to the so-called real business of competitive or alienated life. On the contrary, one can only overcome and supersede philosophy by way of an *internal* kind of criticism, working properly in and through philosophy to its end. By engaging with it one appropriates its lessons, sounds out its weak points and limits, and then one can use this learning to propel oneself beyond this old way of thinking into a new standpoint and beginning. One is looking for a new dawn of culture, but not one that is simply *anti-* the past, anti-philosophical in an untutored way or simply irrational; i.e., irrational rather than post-rational.

It is not a matter of being *un*philosophical then, but of being *post*-philosophical. One could even argue that the trajectory here is post-postmodern in so far as it seems to supersede most forms of the so-called postmodern in philosophy. For what is being advocated is a post-rational, post-representational, post-critical, post-theoretic, post-conceptual, post-deconstructive way of opening receptively to what is, so that Being may reveal itself in a new way and fresh light, in an experientially richer and more aesthetic way (that is, at a more spontaneous and *affective* level, as we shall see in the next chapter). It's more a matter of a certain kind of mood and feeling, an experiential sense of the preciousness of Being, than of an abstract theorising about Being.

While many other philosophers in the Western tradition have attempted to overcome the past and inaugurate some new beginning, there are a couple of rather unique features in Heidegger's method. Firstly, while others, such as Kant, have sought to overcome previous metaphysics, their attempts have not been radical and complete because they have merely replaced some old form of metaphysics with a new form of it that claims to be the rational truth. Hence, they have not initiated a genuinely post-metaphysical and post-philosophical stage of awareness. But Heidegger aims to go beyond all metaphysics, all representational thinking—all 'isms' altogether, we might say. This is to be done by realising our intellectual grasping at reality (as well as our ordinary everydayness and the whole scientific-pragmatic way of thinking) is all part of what generates in us the addictive false consciousness, or fallenness, that obscures the truth, depth, and precious Quality of Being. Hence, the old should be 'sacrificed,' as he sometimes puts it.[10] This voluntary sacrifice of the intellect and will-to-power, this 'abnegation' of the human ego, the old self, the old man, will reveal to us the experiential 'treasure' that lies in being fully open to the truth of Being.

Secondly, Heidegger frequently employs etymological studies of ancient Greek terms as part of his method to support his contentions. So to this we will now turn.

PRE-SOCRATIC PHILOSOPHY

Although the Western tradition in philosophy has led us far from Being, not toward it, things have not always been this way. For, he says, if we go right back to before the very beginnings of the Western tradition, right back to the pre-Socratics, we will discover that those earliest Greek philosophers had a much clearer appreciation and apprehension of Being than we do today. This can be seen, he argues, in their use of the ancient Greek language. We might clarify what he means by looking at two examples.

Take the ancient Greek word for truth: *aletheia*.[11] In ancient Greek mythology, Lethe, the daughter of Eris, was the personification of oblivion. Lethe is also the name given to a river in the underworld. If a people drink of this water, they forget everything or enter into a state of oblivion. The word *lethe* suggested concealment, oblivion and forgetfulness. *A-letheia*, therefore, should suggests the opposite: a remembrance, a recollection, a standing forth into the light of day, a showing forth, an opening forth, an emerging into clearness and appearance, into presence, into the truth of Being. If so, it suggests the opposite of our everyday forgetfulness of our existence and of the truth of Being.

Such an etymological excursion paves the way for Heidegger to argue that for the earliest Greek thinkers 'truth' did not have the meaning that it has for us today—where it usually means the correspondence of propositions (representational thoughts) with beings and/or with one another: thoughts correctly picturing, mirroring or representing reality in words in a coherent system of thoughts and beliefs. Rather, it meant this standing forth of things in and from the Being/Nothingness of their ground or source. To be or live 'in the truth' meant, therefore, to be in that state of recollection that allows one to harken to and witness this standing forth, this presence, in optimum clearness.

Moreover, by the phrase, 'the truth of Being' he means to refer us to this state of clearness whereby beings emerge and stand forth *in and from and in relation to* their source; that is, as rooted in and giving expression to their source in Being. They are not separated and cut off from Being in our thinking but become part of a Being-centred awareness of beings. Or if this is an easier way to put it: things stand forth in the full light of their is-ness, and that is-ness is what we are mainly attending to in this experience of truth. Is-ness, or pure Being as such, is to be experienced in and through the things, and in this way our general involvement with things in the world need not lead to a forgetfulness of Being—not if we are living or standing in the truth.

He can then argue that we, in this epoch, rarely stand in the truth, or rarely live truthfully, in this sense. Our everyday lives are a kind of lie. For we live mainly focused on things, dealing with and gaining things, in the forgetfulness of Being. This Being lies somewhat concealed in a kind of oblivion. We easily lose sight of it. In a moment it slips back into concealment. Usually the light of our attention is not on the factor of Being. For we are usually caught up in enthralment to the things of this world in a temporal pragmatic way, giving them individual value and importance as if separate from Being. Approaching them with this kind of divisive and separative attitude (separating beings from Being) we are focused mainly on how to possess and keep the individual things for ourselves, and how to use and control them for our various egocentric purposes. Thus, we act in our alienation from Being.

Now let's consider the ancient Greek word *logos*—an extremely important word for Western philosophy and religion (one only has to recall the opening of the Gospel of St John, 'In the beginning was the word,'—that is, the *logos*). Logos has been variously translated in the tradition, as 'word,' 'reasoned account' and 'conceptual meaning'. It was also translated into the Latin *ratio* from which we get 'rational' and 'reason'.

Heidegger argues that this is a very misleading translation, one that has generated a wrong emphasis in Western metaphysics on words, reasons, and conceptual meanings.[12] He claims that the word originally derives from the ancient Greek verb *legein,* which he says means 'to collect or arrange together'. In this sense, when things are properly arranged they are set in their proper *context* within which they emerge or stand forth as the things they are. They are then fully present to us, not simply as individual separate things, named as *this* and *that*, but in the sense of things being present-in-their-proper-context. This means that the things of the world, the beings, stand forth in the context of their inseparable relation to Being itself. Thus: they are not seen by us as isolated from Being—used by us in the forgetfulness of Being—for they are seen as present-in-their-Being. Logos, therefore, when understood this way, should refer us to the Being of beings, or to beings standing forth and lying as they are, arranged together in an interconnected way in their proper background context; hence, in the clearness of their Being, inseparable from Being, and at one with Being. We also will be at one with Being in this mode of experience.

If so, it is misleading to translate *logos* as 'reason,' where this is understood in the modern sense of 'giving a reason for something'; that is, giving an intellectual or causal explanation or reasoned account of the existence of something. Looking for such reasons leads us to engage in separative scientific and metaphysical ways of thinking where we try to explain the existence of things intellectually, mathematically and systematically, and we look for prior causes in the time series for everything that comes into existence. Indeed, in this way of thinking we are eventually led all the way back to think about what the *first cause* might be (God, the Big Bang, etcetra) for all the things that come to be. But in so thinking we are dealing continually with beings, things, conceptualised entities—within the circle of beings or this separative way of thinking—and are therefore led away from the authentic awareness of immediate Being Itself. We are seduced and distracted from the immediate presence of beings-in-the-context-of-Being, in the clarity of their Being. We cloud and obscure this clarity with our *logocentric* ways of thinking (when *logos* is translated in the traditional way).

His claim is that the earliest Greek thinkers were not so easily distracted. For when they sought to find the *logos* of something, the *meaning* of something, they were not so concerned with seeking a chain of intellectual reasons, causes, and explanations—a meaning in that sense—but rather with the presence of beings in their Being, and the meaning that could be felt and experienced in the clearness of that apprehension. We might put it this way: the meaning of life and the existence of things is not to be found in intellectual answers, rational systems, causal explanations and the like. It is, rather, to be found in the lucid apprehension and appreciation of beings standing unveiled in their Being, where their is-ness, as it were, shines forth clearly as a strongly sensed presence. Things then stand forth resplendent with Being.[13]

Meaning, value, truth, is then something we feel, experience, or 'stand in', rather than something we think and reason about metaphysically or scientifically. We can't have a metaphysical or scientific answer to the question: What is the meaning of life? We can only *allow* or *let* the meaning unfold for us experientially in contemplative mode, in experiencing the Quality of 'the truth of Being'. The meaning of life will lie in the deep experience of things being *resplendent* with Being; in that kind of *aura* of awe and beauty of Being.

Note how, for the 'new man' Heidegger, the existentialist encounter with nothingness has become an experience of resplendent Being. The earlier angst and dread has been overtaken by a new almost sacred awe and even serenity.[14] The aura of awe and serenity develops from frequently letting go of the human will-to-power and just letting beings show forth in their Being. Thus, in a non-separative way, beyond the old dualism of the ordinary metaphysical thinking so unmindful of the experience of Being and being at one with Being.

It is rather like, say, how one might approach experiencing music. Rather than simply opening receptively and sympathetically to experiencing the music, some people may be habituated or addicted to always thinking about the music with a view to analysing it intellectually or explaining it—asking what the logos of it is (in that sense of the word). They want an intellectual account of the music to thereby grasp its proper meaning in concepts. They are not satisfied unless they can get an intellectual answer, or until they have the reason or idea or blueprint that is thought to lie behind a thing's production. They want the essential idea behind it, the causal explanation, rather than the music itself.

I recall reading somewhere that the composer Jean Julius Sibelius (1865–1957) played the recording of a new Symphony to a friend. When it had finished the friend said, 'Very good, Sibelius. But can you tell me please, *what does your Symphony mean?*' Sibelius was so taken aback by the question that all he could think to do to reply to this person who sought its meaning was to remain silent and play the recording of the Symphony again. The point being: the meaning of the music lies in its presence itself when this is apprehended clearly, without distractions entering in, and when one is at one's most receptive to it. The experiential meaning and quality unfolds of itself, by itself. Likewise, we could say the same about Being, Existence Itself or Life.

The meaning of Being is not to be found in intellectual answers, but in living and experiencing it fully, in the clearing or clearness, attuned to its immediate aesthetic quality, where we let beings be in all the aesthetic splendour of their Being.

EXISTENCE IS UNINTELLIGIBLE

We have mentioned in passing how metaphysical and scientific thinking leads us to look for explanations and causes for the existence of things by looking backwards into the time series for some antecedent idea or temporal cause. Let us explore this a little further now. For Heidegger's discussion of this will bring out an important existentialist point about the approach to the aura of pure Being.

In his book, *The Principle of Reason*, he undertakes a close analysis of the meaning of the principle in philosophy expressed by Leibniz that, 'nothing is without a ground or reason' or 'nothing is without a cause'.[15] Many philosophers have taken this 'principle of sufficient reason' to be fundamental, a *first principle* of all philosophy and science—a necessary foundation for them if they are to make rational sense, and if they are to provide the logos of things in the sense of a reasoned account and explanation of the way things are.

This foundational principle calls us to look for and find the reason or cause behind everything, for only when we have found it, so it is said, will we have an 'adequate' explanation. Only then will existence be rendered intellectually intelligible. Only then will we be able to feel at home in it as intellectual beings, for as such we can only feel at home with what is intellectually intelligible. When the world seems to lack this intelligibility, we tend to feel lost, bewildered, confused, frustrated, uneasy, anxious and alienated from a reality we can't understand, that seems to make no rational sense. If reality defies reason it will seem absurd, inexplicable to us, and we will not be able to find satisfaction in it in the light of this absurdity. Hence, the call of the principle of sufficient reason is a call to render existence meaningful in the sense of intellectually intelligible. That will then enable us to feel reassured about reality, believing that we now *know* how and why it works and is the way it is. Many people are still looking for a Grand Unified Theory to explain everything and so make it seem meaningful to us in this manner.

This aspiration has been a motivating force within the Western philosophical tradition from Plato to Nietzsche (apart from the Pyrrhonian Sceptics, that is, and others influenced by this extreme form of Scepticism). It begins in grand metaphysics (especially Plato) but finds its natural end, according to Heidegger, in the modern sciences. They have taken over this human quest for sufficient reasons and explanations.

However, we might note in passing that a glitch in the system has appeared in recent times insofar as subatomic events appear to defy the principle of sufficient reason. That is, they seem to occur randomly, without apparent reason or cause—at least according to the standard Copenhagen Interpretation of Quantum Physics. This is an interpretation of the nature of reality that Einstein was never able to accept, for he was a true disciple of the principle of sufficient reason: he thought there must be a reason or cause somewhere, somehow, that would rationally explain and account for all such subatomic events. Or as he famously put it, 'God does not play dice'. However, rather oddly and ironically, although science embraces the principle of sufficient reason as its foundational principle, it has departed from Einstein and seems willing nowadays to accept the random nature of subatomic events—at least for the time being anyway—although it cannot offer an 'adequate' explanation of them, that is, in terms of causality and sufficient reasons.

But to return: Heidegger reflects critically on this so-called fundamental principle in various ways, for example, somewhat as follows. It is meant as a *first* principle. But what *is* a first principle? A first principle is said to be that which supplies the reason or ground for something else said to follow from it. A principle contains the reason for what follows from the principle, as does an axiom. And this first principle is saying just this: that everything must refer to some prior ground or reason or principle or cause for its existence. There must be some basic principle that explains the existence of a thing.

But then, in that case, what of this first principle itself? What is the ground or reason or principle for asserting *this* as a first principle? What does it itself 'follow from'? This first principle, it would seem, must have another principle even more fundamental than it is in order to provide a reason or ground for it. Now, we are here into either an infinite regress of principles, or else we have to assert, rather arbitrarily, that something just is the first principle and that it does not have anything grounding it. However, this contradicts the very idea expressed in the principle itself; namely, that everything must have a principle or reason or ground. Thus, it seems we fall into the groundless: we find that this 'first principle' is not grounded by any prior principle more fundamental than it, and yet that it cannot ground itself, or provide a sufficient reason for itself. We begin to realise that ultimately there is no reason why 'everything must have a reason,' or why we must *assume* this to be the case.[16]

This is quite remarkable. And it is a good point that can be raised against anything taken to be a first principle, or reason, or cause or ground. For example, there is a similar paradox encountered in what is traditionally called *The Cosmological Argument for the Existence of God*. Similar to the Principle of Sufficient Reason, the Cosmological Argument states there must be a reason or cause for everything that exists, for every effect. The universe itself, as a totality, must have a cause, and one that is not contained within it, since it is a cause that explains the occurrence of the totality. This cause, standing outside the universe as the first cause of it, is then said to be God. We are then supposed to conclude rationally that God exists as the first cause of everything.

The usual response to this argument is to raise the question: If the principle of the argument here is that everything must have a cause or reason to account for its existence and that, therefore, God is what accounts for the universe, then what accounts for God? That is, if everything must have a cause then what causes God? Once again we seem to be caught here in an infinite regress. For if we say that there is a cause for the existence of God, then we will be pushed back a stage further and we will ask: And what is the cause of the cause that causes God? And so on. Alternatively, we might insist on drawing the line at God, rather arbitrarily, and we will say: God is self-causing. God causes Himself to exist. However, this either makes no sense in so far as it implies that God must exist *first* in order to be able to cause Himself (or Herself, if you prefer) to exist, or else it says that God simply exists and always has done, and does so *without a cause, without a reason*, precisely in defiance of the very principle on which the Cosmological Argument is based, namely, that everything must have a cause or reason or ground for its existence. (The same argument can be applied to the concept of a Big Bang as an ultimate explanation).

This is not merely an academic exercise. The implication of it is this: that when we think things out clearly and press the basic premises of our rational thought about the world far enough, we find that our quest for the intellectual intelligibility of everything—as expressed, for example, in the Principle of Sufficient Reason—breaks down at some point (and not only at the subatomic level). We seek intellectual intelligibility by seeking the reason or ground of things, and yet there is a point at which we arrive at *groundlessness*; a complete lack of ultimate causes or explanations. Existence as a whole is exposed as *unintelligible*: the quest for intelligibility fails. Ultimately, existence is groundless and inexplicable, so we may as well begin to face up authentically to this fact instead of obscuring it with rationalist assumptions and pursuits.

The point here is similar to one made by Kierkegaard: every metaphysical system must start from some leap of faith—or as we might prefer to say—some arbitrary decision to take something, some so-called first principle, as final or ultimate, and our essential starting point for inquiry. For the *first* principle of a rational system of explanation cannot itself be supposed to be accounted for by some other or prior principle, else it wouldn't be the *first* principle. But no first principle can establish itself or ground itself, for then we would be arguing in a circle and simply begging the question at issue, hence bluntly *assuming* the validity of the first principle to get the argument underway. Therefore, it logically follows: *no system can ground itself or establish itself as the rational truth.*

This point has become a standard existentialist argument against all objective systems and truths, or against what we called 'the power of objectivity' in chapter three. The upshot is that existence remains intellectually unintelligible and the traditional quest of both metaphysics and science to explain things appears futile in the end.

Heidegger also points out that first principles are *axioms*. But, of course, he claims that this word, in its modern usage, fails to capture the original meaning of the ancient Greek source, *axio,* a verb meaning 'to value' or 'appreciate' something.[17] For example, the word *axiology* means the study of values. Strictly speaking, and originally, an *axiom* refers us to something, some principle, which is held in the highest esteem or regard—that which is *valued* as supreme. It is not that an *axiom* is something simply given as the rational truth, or that which *must* be taken as a first principle to think and live by. Rather, we have to value it first and thereby *choose* it.

This point seems similar to one made by Nietzsche when he said, 'Behind all logic there stands evaluation'. The implication is that there is something more fundamental than reason and logic or all rational thinking about the world and that is evaluation; hence, the subjective choice of an approach to life or set of values and meanings. It is only through an act of subjective evaluation that we come to regard or count certain so-called 'first principles' or 'axioms' as being essential and authoritative for us.

For example, take even reason itself. How can it be established that using reason is the right way to live or approach reality, or the right tool to use to discover truth? This has been assumed to be the case by most philosophers in the past, and in modern times and it is simply taken for granted by them—so much so that the question of the value of reason and truth was rarely asked prior to existentialism. Why should we live rationally? How can reason ground itself or validate itself? If we say that reason is validated by a prior principle that is itself pre-rational or non-rational, then we get back into an infinite regress again. On the other hand, if we say that reason validates itself we argue in a circle and beg the question at issue—or we simply make an arbitrary decision to accept reason as valid or self-validating and take this for our first principle, our highest court of appeal, our supreme authority in life.

In short, most philosophers and all scientists as such have arbitrarily decided to value reason as their authority, even although nothing can validate this choice and other choices are equally possible and equally valid (or invalid). For example, some people may arbitrarily decide to value something other than reason; their mystical or spiritual feelings, intuitions and experiences or perhaps the Bible, Vedas, etcetera, and take that as their supreme authority.

Let's remember that Martin Luther (1483–1546), for example, regarded human reason as the devil's whore and considered it a corrupt faculty, an aspect of our sinful and fallen human nature. Without guidance from scriptural revelation, it leads us *away* from the truth, not *toward* it. Therefore, from this point of view, an 'age of reason' or 'the age of the enlightenment' cannot be regarded as progress. Nor can it be said that science leads to progress or civilisation, or that science progresses toward truth or a greater approximation to real knowledge. To properly progress and get to the truth we must defer to the Bible, Luther would say, not to unguided human reason alone. If the Bible should at any point conflict with human reason or empirical evidence? Well then, so much the worse for human reason and science! We should always go by the revealed word of God; it is more reliable than reason or empirical evidence. So speaks the people of faith. The people of an alternative faith—that is, the rationalists and scientists and enlightenment thinkers—fail to answer this point or even address it. They cannot answer it, so they ignore it. That is a perfect example of the intellectual subterfuge that *they* complain of in the arguments of religious believers!

Try asking yourself, 'What is my criterion of truth?' By what standard or measure do you decide what is ultimately true or false *for you*? How would you justify it, if challenged? One example of a criterion of truth that has been very popular in the past and has been proposed as a fundamental first principle is The Verification Principle of the Truth. This is the principle that only those propositions that can be verified through repeatable empirical testing by scientific procedures are to be regarded as true, while statements, say, of aesthetics or ethics, statements expressive of personal values, are to be thought of merely as expressions of human emotion, as the early twentieth century moral philosophy *Emotivism* says. Such expressions of emotion are neither objectively true nor false. And metaphysical statements that are not empirically testable by scientific procedures? They are to be regarded as meaningless!

But now, the question can be asked: Is the Verification Principle proved true because it is verifiable? If you say yes, then the principle merely presupposes its own validity, and so you beg the question at issue by assuming the truth of that which is to be proved. Or if you say it is not, then by what *other* criterion of truth is the Verification Principle shown to be true? This line of thought will lead us back into an infinite regress of criteria.

It is easy to see that the same type of argument can be applied to *any* criterion of truth that anyone proposes. If it is supposed to prove itself then it assumes its own validity and one is merely arguing in a circle. But if it does not, then it must appeal to another principle or criterion and one is off into the infinite regress. The upshot is: no criterion of truth can be shown to be the correct one. But if no criterion of truth can be established, how then can we have any truth? And then, how could it even be argued that it is true that there is no truth? Once again thought is *stymied*. It's worse than a Zen koan!

POETIC PLAY

Perhaps Heidegger himself does not express it in quite these terms, but he seems to think something similar, that traditional philosophical thinking does not get us anywhere. It needs to be overcome because even as basic a principle as the Principle of Sufficient Reason lacks solid grounds and seems self-defeating. In his aforementioned book, *The Principle of Reason*, he contrasts the idea that everything must have a reason or ground with a verse from the poem *The Cherubinic Wanderer* by the mystical poet Angelus Silesius (1624–1677):

> The rose is without why;
> It blooms because it blooms;
> It cares not for itself, asks not if it is seen.[18]

One could read the poet as saying the rose ultimately has no reason or ground for its existence. It is 'without why,' for its ultimate ground is the groundless ground of Being itself, which is without why. When the rose is experienced clearly, in its proper context—in its truth (in this sense)—it is experienced as resplendent with Being and we accept it in all its glory as being in Being without why.[19]

We need look no further than this for the truth of the rose. Indeed, if we do look further, that is, for rational or causal explanations for the rose being as it is, this will tend to cloud over and obscure the resplendent Being of the rose. We will no longer be seeing the rose in the clearness of its relation to groundless Being, but seeing it in a temporal and linear way in its relation to causal antecedents in time; hence, technically, scientifically, metaphysically. Moreover, we will be isolating the rose as an object for intellectual analysis and study, separating it off from Being Itself, as if it existed separately. The more poetic alternative is to contemplate the rose without this intellectual analysis and separative thought. Hence, just letting it be in Being, as revealing Being. We may find that when we contemplate the rose in this way that the beauty and glory of the Being of the rose reveals itself to us more fully, more intensely, more gloriously. We may even have an awed sense of the sacred aura of the rose, of the preciousness of its being as an expression of Being. That is, not as an isolated thing lacking rootedness, but as it points back to its source.

The rose, of course, can also be used as a poetic symbol for the world as such. So the poet may be showing us here how we might look at *all things*; not just flowers or things usually regarded as beautiful. If we open ourselves to experiencing everything or anything as the poet experiences the rose, as a being in Being without why, just so, then potentially any object of contemplation might stand forth for us resplendent with Being. So any object as such may reveal its aura of beauty and glory—as seen in this, its proper context—if one can open to it 'in truth' in this more poetic or aesthetic way.

However, this is not to say that we must always avoid representational thinking or intellectual analysis or the pursuit of this kind of 'provisional intelligibility' of things. That is, one is not saying all scientific or pragmatic thinking must be forever set aside. Rather, there is a time and place for these different approaches. At another time, it might be appropriate to analyse the rose, seeking out its causes or understanding its evolution or molecular structure, for example. But the poem is reminding us that the pragmatic attitude that tends to dominate in our modern culture and that obscures the importance of experiencing Being without why, is not the only or the most important approach to take to life. Indeed, a more poetic and contemplative approach may be more valid and more beneficial to us.

Let us consider the validity question first. One might say it seems more valid because Heidegger's discourse has shown that the ordinary, representational, metaphysical, and pragmatic way of thinking that seeks the temporal causal ground and explanation for everything, ultimately fails to find any final ground or first ground or cause or explanation. So it seems explanations fail in the end and everything remains ultimately ungrounded. Now we might perhaps say that the ground of all beings is Being, that this is the ultimate source of their existence. But Being has no ground: for we cannot find any first cause of it. Therefore, *ultimately things just are; just so*. So, more often than we do, we might just let them *be there* in their Being without why and cease asking for grounds and explanations all the time.

CREATIVITY

We should more often let beings be in the truth of their Being, that is, in their groundless ground, in groundlessness. Thus we will remain true to our insight into the *voidness* of grounds—shunyata.

This could be considered an existentially authentic way to be. Moreover, we should also note that we ourselves, as human beings, are beings, and so we ourselves lack grounds: we are part of this groundless situation of life. So to be existentially authentic in relation to this realisation, we would often contemplate our own being as without why, just like the rose.

What now about the question of the benefit? Will it be beneficial for us to be without why? Well, what does it mean to be without why? It means that, as a consequence of having had some insight into its voidness and futility, one gives up on the ordinary metaphysical thinking about existence and no longer wasting one's time and energy on this rather self-defeating quest that has so often occupied and preoccupied people in the past; indeed, driving them quite crazy and leading to some quite crazy disputes too, even fanatical wars.

Also, in allowing Being to be without why, we are letting go of our old need for final answers and intellectual explanations for everything; for this kind of 'closure'. In this way we will no longer be so bothered and frustrated by our failure to find the said answers—this frustration being a form of our disquiet (*duhkha*). In fact, we can soon discover that such answers are not required after all to develop a peace of mind, a deep sense of meaning in life or inspiring sense of the rich aesthetic quality of life.

Also, having given up on this grasping for answers, we become much more attuned and open to things as they are, just so, in their immediacy and presence, in their simple is-ness without why. And in this state of mind we discover a certain depth, a rich experiential quality, an aura, a beauty and grace, a wonderment of Being that may have hitherto escaped us. Moreover, in this state of sympathetic openness and receptivity, we become, rather like the mystical poets, more open to the subtle creative promptings and intuitions of Being. That is, *harkening* to Being we may feel something like an inner voice, or a muse, guiding us, or addressing us, helping to clarify, transform, and create a new way of thinking; a type of thinking that takes Being or Nothing as its primary point of departure and reference rather than separate things or selves, as in the old paradigm.

Heidegger calls this new way of thinking, 'poetic and meditative thinking'.[20] So what he seems to be advocating here, as a post-metaphysical, post-critical, post-philosophical way of being in the world, is that we practice a more meditative, more silent and still, contemplative approach to life that can give rise to a more poetic style of thinking—one rooted in the open and still experience of Being and that does not operate in the old way, in forgetfulness of Being. The stillness speaks, as it were. (This approach may also remind us of that *other* Eckhart—namely, Eckhart Tolle—and his books, *The Power of Now* and *Stillness Speaks*).

Heidegger takes the word he uses for this practice from Meister Eckhart: *gelassenheit*, which can be translated as 'letting go and letting be'.[21] It requires the kind of receptive openness to beings-in-their-Being that we have been talking about—although Meister Eckhart, as a Christian mystic, also speaks of this as a matter of seeing creatures in their Creator (in whom they live and breath and have their being, etc) or as a case of seeing God in everything—seeing *divinity* in everything. Everything is holy, etcetera. But this is, nevertheless, somewhat similar to saying we see the beings-in-their-Being, as resplendent in Being, and thereby experience and appreciate 'the treasure,' the preciousness of their Being. It is Being that is the ultimate 'precious,' not this or that object taken in isolation. However, when we see objects, not in isolation, as if separate from Being, but in existential relation to their source, the wholeness of Being, then the objects tend to take on a certain precious quality too as reflective and expressive of Being. We will not seek out particular people or things as separately 'my precious'—like Gollum's famous ring—and fall into fetishism or idolatry, but rather look to see how everyone and everything can be precious together in the abode of Being.

Angelus Silesius, who was influenced by Meister Eckhart, also puts it in *The Cherubinic Wanderer* that, 'God plays with His creatures. It is all a game that God is playing'. And Caputo elaborates on this:

> Creatures originate in God, not as in a first cause, but as in a being who out of His own superabundance and good-ness, needing nothing outside of Himself, has freely and spontaneously chosen to communicate Being to them. Creation is a game God plays for His own pleasure. And the creature who would make his way back to God must employ not 'words' but 'play'... The relation between God and the soul is a dialectic of playing, a game of love and grace. It is neither a metaphysical-causal nor an ethical-juridical relation.[22]

In other words, our lives are not to be understood in terms of a moral fall and redemption, with souls awaiting judgement at the end of days, nor are we to think of God as a first cause in a series of causes in the temporal order. Rather God would be timeless Being itself and creation would be God's temporal theatre of play—for amusement, diversity of experience and the beauty of art and drama—not as a 'moral testing ground' for individual souls with freewill. Moreover, Caputo points out that a similar idea is employed by Heidegger with regard to Being. For Heidegger says that causal reasoning, the why and the because, 'is swallowed up in the play. It plays because it plays. There remains only play: the highest and the deepest.'[23] Moreover, the play of Being is as inscrutable as a child at play. 'The mission of Being: a child who plays,' says Heidegger.[24] Life is the spontaneous play of Being without why. Max Stirner quotes the lines:

> I sing as the bird sings
> That on the bough alights;
> The song that from me springs
> Is play that well requites.[25]

One sings simply because one is a singer. One sings in the self-enjoyment of singing. One does not have to have a why. One does not have to be doing it for any ulterior purpose or reason, but just in and for itself. For play requires no why or purpose outside itself. Likewise, God or Being creates without why, as pure play. We come closest to this ourselves when we live and create and play without why, as in a timeless moment, that is sufficient unto itself. Our action will be play, an engaged disengagement in the temporal theatre of the world.

Now this may give some people moral unease. However, be patient, more will be said on ethics in the next chapter. For the present though we can say this. There is indeed something morally questionable about the idea of God 'playing with His creatures' if we assume the usual metaphysics of representational thinking, namely, that divisive ontology that separates beings from beings and even refers to God as a separate being, for example, as the first cause in accordance with the principle of sufficient reason. For then God would be imposing this world play—including all the pains of life it involves—upon us as separate and vulnerable beings. That would surely be a form of tyranny: an infliction of suffering and death on separate others without any kind of informed consent.

However, precisely this dualistic metaphysical thinking is undermined in both Eckhart and Heidegger. God is not a separate being for Eckhart: God and the self are one. One's innermost self, the true I, is God. Also, for Heidegger, there is no ontological separation of selves from Being, since that idea is part of the ordinary representational thinking of beings in separation from Being that is suspended in the clearing that enables true openness to Being. Therefore, there is no ontological dualism here. There is no independent and tyrannical God imposing world play or pain on others. It is the one Joyful Player that is playing and the one Joyful Player is *both the creator and the one experiencing everything*. There is no separation. In short, we can arrive at something like this verse:

> Maya, Maya,
> All this world is but a play
> Be thou the joyful player![26]

At any rate, we in our existential freedom can elect to see it this way as our own poetic preference. We would create the world as our own theatre and our innermost Self as the one timeless Joyful Player. This more poetic, playful, theatrical and contemplative way of life may be the best way to recover our sense of being at one with Life or Being, being at home in Life or Being, fully belonging to Life or Being without separation or alienation, and of finding the experience aesthetically rich, pleasing and rewarding. With this we regain our sense of the Quality, meaning, and value of Life or Being—even regain 'the truth' of Being (in the contemplative and poetic sense of the word). If so, we would no longer feel as anxious and estranged from everything as we did in the time of our 'existential malaise'. We would become one with the Joyful Player.

This may be the best way to overcome and supersede our modern or postmodern age, an age in which we were enthralled by separative human reason and the alienated will-to-power—especially as it was expressed through technology and the abuse of the environment, compulsive consumerism, ruthless competitiveness, economic rationalism and the authoritarian imposition of ideological systems. It may also be the way to cure ourselves of the old world-weariness of endless critical theory and nihilism, the sense of lostness, the frustration of failing to find intellectual answers while still being addicted to looking for them and that uneasy feeling that our lives lack lasting significance, rootedness, meaning and value. The twentieth century's existential disease, arising as a result of the whole preceding tradition of Western philosophy with its failures and futilities, can be cured in a new dawn, a new beginning, a revitalisation of the culture, a renewal that will be mainly based, not on the intellectual and critical analysis of ontologically separate beings, but on the experiencing of beings in their ontological interrelatedness in the theatrical world-play of unified life.

Instead of seeing everything and everyone divisively, as separate and isolated, existing in hostile opposition, in conflict, and in disharmony, we see everything and everyone as fundamentally interconnected, as one, all cooperatively playing their parts together in the whole play. All the parts in the one play are equally important, equally valued, equally precious and included, and even the relatively bad parts, the so-called evils in life, work together with the good parts for the overall artistic fulfilment of the whole play. Instead of seeing discord everywhere, we see harmony everywhere. Instead of seeing life at odds with itself, we see life complementing itself.

Our turn around here has been in effect a turning away from Nietzsche's antagonistic and competitive will-to-power to open instead to the gracious power of what is; voided, of course, of particular names and conceptualisations. In effect: Being or Nothingness seen in the uncanny light of shunyata. It is a call to aesthetic contemplation and a call away from merely exercising the power of our existential subjectivity in thoughts and actions.

However, as suggested at the end of the last chapter, we need not insist on the one at the complete expense of the other. For what might be best of all is a kind of dynamic balancing and spiralling interplay between the two. Thus: in our moments of empowered free subjectivity emancipated from the power of objectivity we can elect to poetically affirm and reaffirm the wholeness of what is, and so poetically affirm the totality as the one transcendental, transpersonal, artistic Player, who plays the world like a child at play and hence, as a divine source worthy of our time and contemplation. In our moments of contemplation we may discover, more experientially than intellectually, some spontaneous and authentic mood and feeling of the goodness and beauty of this timeless playing we call the world.

The deep and rich affective beauty of the experience of naked isness can inspire us, and then this inspiration can feed back into the free subjective affirmation of the wholeness of what is as the artwork of the one Player, with our human egos as the various personas of the

pleasure

one Player. It helps ground and support the poetic vision with an aesthetic feeling and mood. Meanwhile the free subjective holistic affirmation of life as the artwork of the one Player can create a positive intellectual framework (as a fallible commitment of course) that is appropriate to, and supportive of, the timeless experience of voided aesthetic contemplation. In this way, the two processes can aid one another in an evolving spiral, a kind of double game.

The double game is a matter of playing with the free subjective affirmation of poetic thought and action in the moment of reflection, and of playing with the voided contemplation of timeless and nameless is-ness in the moment of de-reflection. There is an engaged disengagement in both; hence, they are both modes of play and one can learn to instantaneously alternate between them. It is like a kind of neo-Stirnerian, neo-Nietzschean affirmation and self-enjoyment of the wholeness of life, combined with a Buddhist-like meditative voidance. In other words, there is an active and holistic *via positiva* of the one divine Player and a radical *via negativa* of passive contemplation, with both playing together in the way of an alternating engaged disengagement.

This new style of existential thinking, a meditative and poetic thinking, will constantly return us to the practice of *gelassenheit*—letting go and letting be without why, being nobody, going nowhere—that characterises the life of void contemplation and poetic play. We will return to this again and again as our wellspring of peace, beauty, and joy, as in and from voidance we continue to venture to affirm a free subjective 'Yes' to the ideal and overall existential perfection of *what is*, as it is, just so as it unfolds, here and now, in this world. At any rate, we are free to do this until or unless someone can prove to us that reality is essentially otherwise than ideal and perfect. Until then, let us continue to poetically create and annul the unified real as ideal, just as we please.

Not in the competitive pursuit of material wealth and the possession of particular beings and powers considered separately precious as fetish objects and idols, but in playing in this double game of void aesthetic contemplation and free poetic thought, will we find our source of wholesome wellness and wellbeing in life. All will be well with our being when we let our being shine forth in life without why and we use this rich aesthetic experience to help us recreate and re-affirm the holistic value of what is as the one play of the divine Player.

In sum: the double game is the way to move from the state of alienated angst to the state of harmonious interconnected play and the aesthetic re-enchantment of life.

HOLISTIC BEAUTY AND LOVE

Because love is the unknown, we must come to it by discarding the
known. The unknown cannot be discovered by a mind that is full
of the known.
— Jiddu Krishnamurti

AESTHETICS IS THAT branch of Western philosophy that studies theories of art, creativity and beauty. In Aesthetics, the notion of 'the aesthetic attitude' has often been discussed. The philosopher Immanuel Kant gave considerable impetus to the idea, by way of his analysis of the aesthetic contemplation of free beauty in the first part of his third critique, his classic text, *The Critique of Judgement*.[1] Two more recent sources on the topic are more accessible for the ordinary reader: a book of the lectures and essays of the Cambridge philosopher Edward Bullough (1880–1934), entitled *Aesthetics*,[2] and a book by the philosopher Jerome Stolnitz (b. 1925) called *Aesthetics and the Philosophy of Art Criticism*.[3] Crucial to our discussion in this chapter, is the section from this entitled 'The Aesthetic Attitude'. This important section has been reprinted in John Hospers, *Introductory Readings In Aesthetics*[4] and again in Carolyn Korsmeyer, *Aesthetics: The Big Questions*.[5]

In Jerome Stolnitz's book, the notion of the aesthetic attitude plays a central role in his account of the experience of beauty and the 'free delight'—as Kant calls it[6]—that this kind of experience spontaneously quickens in us. Stolnitz proposes to explain aesthetic experience, aesthetic perception and aesthetic sensitivity, in terms of this pure aesthetic attitude.

He begins by observing that 'attitude' in general is of crucial significance when it comes to how we experience the world and things around us. For *what* we see and *how* we see it is very largely determined by the kind of attitude we have. As he says:

> An attitude is a way of directing and controlling our perception. We never see or hear anything in the environment indiscriminately. Rather, we 'pay attention' to some things, whereas we apprehend others only dimly or hardly at all. Thus attention is selective—it concentrates on some features of our surroundings and ignores others.[7]

This accords well with the view one usually finds in modern psychology texts on perception, namely, that it is rather inaccurate to think of the human being as merely a pure receiver who simply absorbs the stimuli in the environment and then interprets it. Rather, there is always some element of active selection, albeit often subconscious, in our perception of things. We approach the environment with some kind of attitude and intention through which certain aspects are singled out for our attention in relation to our various purposes. The attitude and intention will affect what gets selected and how we see it. Consequently, when people have different attitudes, purposes, intentions, biases, etcetera, they will naturally perceive the world differently. It is not simply that they interpret things differently *after* they have been perceived, but that they actually *perceive* them differently from the first. Perception is not neutral. Many common psychological tests in relation to perception serve to support this point (see Richard L. Gregory's *Eye And Brain*).[8]

Stolnitz mentions the example of the Indian Scout who gives very close attention to markings and clues on the forest floor that the non-Indian, who is simply strolling through the woods, will completely miss and just not *see* at all.[9] So we might add: a great deal of what we perceive in the environment, and how we perceive it, or what we fail to perceive, is culturally determined through our attitude, our language, habits, values and biases. People from different cultures can experience the world differently.

Our attitude and intention will also influence, not only what we see and how we see it, but also how we spontaneously respond to what we see—with fear, with anger, with indifference, with purposeful action, negatively or positively, etcetera. For example, as therapists studying depressed patients have often pointed out, the depressed patient not only typically *thinks* in exaggeratedly negative ways, but will actually *perceive* the negative things in the environment selectively, in accordance with his or her mental bias, and of course, *respond* to them negatively also.[10]

The attitude and intention that most often influences our perception and experience of the environment is pragmatically purposive: we tend to see things in terms of their usefulness to us for achieving the temporal and practical goals we set ourselves. For example, we see the pen on the desk as something to pick up and write with; we see the approaching car on the street as something to avoid and so on. As Heidegger would put it, in this everyday pragmatic way of being-in-the-world, objects are there ready-to-hand, and we are immersed with them there, not standing separate or aloof. Heidegger would also point out that there is another common way of being-in-the-world in which objects appear to us quite differently.

We might call this the intellectual-theoretic mode to contrast it with the everyday practical mode. In the intellectual-theoretic mode the immediate practical utility of the thing in front of us is not the focus of attention; rather, we take a step back, as it were, from our practical involvement with things to think abstractly about them, to theorise about them in a relatively detached way. In this way of being-in-the-world objects are revealed as objects for study and intellectual analysis. We are concerned now with how they stand in relation to other objects—with regard to their temporal causal relationships, how the objects come to be as they are and so forth.

THE AESTHETIC ATTITUDE

Neither of these two common attitudes or ways of being-in-the-world—the practical and theoretic—corresponds to the pure aesthetic attitude. So what is this? Stolnitz offers the following concise definition: to practice the aesthetic attitude is to practice, 'a disinterested and sympathetic attention to, and contemplation of, any object of awareness whatever, for its own sake alone'.[11]

He admits the definition may be a little vague as yet. However, if we follow his method of going on to examine the main terms of the definition in more detail we will be able to clarify the key points. I will also add some remarks of my own to make the definition more comprehensive. So let us now consider the main terms.

1 DISINTERESTED

Pure disinterest—we might note in passing that one way to understand and translate Meister Eckhart's key terms *von abgescheidenheit* (disinterest, detachment) and *gelassenheit* (letting go and letting be)—is in terms of pure disinterestedness.[12]

For Stolnitz, disinterestedness means that, when we are practising the aesthetic attitude, we are not looking at the object of awareness with any concern at all for any particular temporal purpose it may serve. We are not intending to utilise the object to further our self-interests, nor manipulate it, or control it, or possess it, nor to enter into strategic calculations about it, nor to appraise and compare it relative to other objects to further our practical ends. Nor do we have an intellectual or theoretical or critical interest or self-interest in the object. That is, we are not intending to analyse or think about the object of awareness in any way, including any scientific or meta-physical or speculative or deconstructive way, nor are we intending to label, or cognise or know it as being this or that object or this or that type of thing.

We are not intending to interpret or name it even. We are suspending the intellectual and linguistic faculty of the mind and simply 'letting the object be,' thus apprehending its being for its own sake while quietly and intently attending to it in its sheer presence or is-ness and in all its intricate and precise details. Rather than *act upon* the object of awareness we are content to let the object *act on us*; that is, *affect* us if it will or can. Being spontaneously affected by the obj-ect—an *affect*, an *emotional* response—is what is meant by the word 'aesthetic' in this context and by this definition. The aesthetic mom-ent is that pure moment in which we are affected, or in which, as we might also say, we spontaneously discover some degree of affection for the object. As Stolnitz puts it:

> We may say of all these non-aesthetic interests and of practical perception generally, that the object is app-rehended with an eye to its origins and consequences, its interrelations with other things. By contrast, the aesthetic attitude isolates the object and focuses upon it—the 'look' of the rocks, the sound of the ocean, the colours in the painting. Hence the object is not seen in a fragmentary or passing manner, as it is in 'practical' perception, e.g., in using a pen for writing. Its whole nature and character are dwelt upon... For the aesthetic attitude things are not to be classified or studied or judged.[13]

According to this definition, what is called 'aesthetic judgement', including art criticism, whereby we actually formulate some propo-sitions about the object of awareness—even a simple comment such as 'this is beautiful'—is something that may occur a moment after the pure aesthetic moment of experience, but strictly speaking it represents a move away from the pure aesthetic moment in itself. For as a simple waiting and letting be, a suspended moment, and a moment of affect or affection, the pure aesthetic moment is devoid of intellectual analysis or judgement as such. Moreover, if we want to maintain and prolong the purity of this mode of aesthetic contemplation we must refrain from resorting to intellectual or critical judgements about the object of awareness for as long as feasible and just savour its effect on our passions or affections.

Now, although we have been speaking here about the importance of disinterest, we need not conclude that in this form of the aesthetic attitude, we are disinterested in every sense of the word, or in the sense of being emotionally cold, dispassionate, aloof, unmoved or simply *un*interested. For we are certainly very interested in the object itself, in letting it be, and we may be very moved and affected by it. Perhaps it would be clearer to say, in the aesthetic attitude, we are at that precise moment, disinterested in practical, intellectual or other non-aesthetic purposes, but that we are nevertheless *very interested in being disinterested* in this way and in maintaining this disinterested attitude; that is, in *dwelling* in this state of pure contemplation of the sheer presence of the object.

In other words, we *do* have an interest here, we are *aesthetically* interested, interested in contemplating the object for itself, letting it be as it is in its sheer presence, in its naked is-ness, and in allowing it to affect us at a feeling level. This interest can be quite passionate in its nature. For we can have quite a passion for 'letting beings be' or 'waiting upon' them to discover if they may affect us aesthetically. If or when they do, that can also arouse certain other passions or inspirations in us.

Therefore, although the pure aesthetic attitude may be called disinterested, and it is in certain senses, it is not dispassionate or emotionally cold. We are just relatively disinterested at that moment in the usual interests, self-interests, passions and emotions we have in acting upon objects to manipulate them in some way for our practical or temporal purposes. We don't succumb to those temporal desires and emotions, but let them go in a kind of timeless moment—a moment unconcerned with the temporal, with the passage of time, with practical goals in time.

2 SYMPATHETIC

The element of sympathy in this definition of the aesthetic attitude refers to how we prepare ourselves to be responsive: to be fully and receptively *opened* to the object of awareness in its immediate presence. If we approach the object of awareness with this attitude, we are very willing and ready to attend closely and mindfully to it for the sake of its own unique features just as they are. We are willing to see it clearly in all its fine details, all other interests suspended. We are willing to allow it to be there for us exactly as it is without alteration, addition or so-called improvement. We must be receptively open to the object in heart and mind, giving it a quiet, sympathetic, positive regard, being prepared to 'accept it on its own terms,' as Stolnitz says. We embrace the being of the object.

To do this properly we will have to critically void any unsympathetic biases we may initially have toward the object of awareness; that is, put aside our prejudgements about it. In short, we put aside any cultural or personal prejudices we may be harbouring against the object 'as is'. We should not resort to a negative bias, negative conditioning in regard to the objects of awareness, as that will block the experience. Rather, we are to be liberal-minded and liberal-hearted or open-minded and open-hearted, in relation to the object just as it is, just so. For only in this way will we be really able to 'harken to' the object for itself, by properly listening to it or observing it closely. Only in this way do we 'give it chance' to penetrate our shell—our usual pragmatism and temporal egocentrism—and so *let* it us affect us aesthetically. We have to allow the object *in*, as it were.

For example, an anti-religious person, a passionate atheist, may have trouble being able to aesthetically appreciate a religious painting or piece of music if he or she allows a critical ideological bias to impede the experience. The person will then be approaching the object with an inappropriate attitude: the attitude and intention to judge the object intellectually from an ideological standpoint. Being so absorbed and wrapped up in a cloud of ideology, the person will not be able to see or hear clearly enough to experience the object for what it is just by itself, in its simple is-ness. Similarly, a person with a strong moralistic bias may not be able to be fully open to an art object such as a sexually explicit photograph because he or she will not simply let it be there as it is, but immediately wants to judge it from a moral point of view as something morally good and salutary, or as something wicked and corrupting, etcetera. The person's intentions will be moralistic then, not purely aesthetic.

Ideology distorts aesthetics. Thought blinkers it. For then, at that moment, we are being intellectuals, not aesthetes. Ideological or critical or deconstructive people, etcetera., if they are unable to set aside their intellectual habits for the moment, may be unable to see any value in certain objects—simple paintings, blood, dirt, ants, the crown jewels, the Taj Mahal, bright clothes, a plastic bag blowing in the wind, a pile of bricks, etcetera—because they are unable or unwilling to be appropriately and fully opened to the thing just as it is, for its own sake, and view it in a purely aesthetic way, which by our definition means a non-intellectual way, or perhaps better, a *post*-intellectual way. They don't have the ideology-free 'suspense of judgement' or 'sympathetic receptivity' required for this mode of experience. In the twentieth century, in particular, ideological intentions, projects and commitments have often distorted and impeded the purest mode of aesthetic contemplation and the aesthetic *affect* that might otherwise arise in relation to the various objects of awareness. Stolnitz says:

> People sometimes remonstrate with a friend who seems to reject offhand works of which they are fond, 'You don't even give it a chance'. To be 'sympathetic' in aesthetic experience means to give the object the 'chance' to show how

it can be interesting to perception.[14]

Perhaps we should say, to show if it *can* be aesthetically affecting, because we must not prejudge the matter, but simply *wait and see*. We should not assume, however, that if it does not show its beauty—or itself resplendent with Being, if you will—that it does not have this beauty. For it may just be that it is we who are not clear, unbiased, open, sympathetically attentive and aesthetically receptive enough. In short, we may be too intellectual, too critical, prejudiced, too blocked. We may not be sufficiently practised in *gelassenheit*, in pure disinterested observation, in letting go and letting be.

3 ATTENTION

Clear disinterested attention first of all requires us to be very wakeful and alert, sharp and focused, open in mind and heart, and able to remain free from being 'dispersed' in any absorbing desires and distractions, or any intellectual interference. We must be able to be 'recollected' from thought-centred, word-centred, time-centred enthralments and preoccupations. We must 'call ourselves back' from all such wayward distractions to be in the clearness, which means that we return ourselves from the fogginess generated in the mind and heart by non-aesthetic temporal interests entering in—our ideological interests, moral interests, utilitarian interests, sexual interests, cognitive interests, critical-deconstructive interests and so forth.

To keep our consciousness bright and clear, as well as relaxed and yet alert, we will have to temporarily place our other interests 'under a cloud of forgetting,' as it were, to borrow a phrase from the mystics.[15] Restless everyday thought, in particular, is a common source of distraction, like a constant static in the mind. So we will need to learn to practice being relatively quiet, recollected, still and inwardly silent. Strictly speaking, a proper practice of the aesthetic attitude is going to require, in effect, a kind of meditative practice of freedom from thought and desire.

Also, to help the practice of aesthetic attention along one may try to 'feel into' the object, as for example, in experiencing music, one may let the body move with the music, sway to the rhythm, tap to the beat and so on, or in contemplating an art object, one may not only look at it, but touch and caress it, run one's fingers along its edges, feel its texture and so forth. One may view the object of awareness from different and novel angles, focus on different parts of it and note some hitherto unnoticed detail or relationship between parts. In such simple ways one may be able to hone and heighten one's aesthetic attention and sympathetic receptivity to the object.

Moreover, aesthetic attention may be heightened and enriched by having some prior training and acquaintance in relation to the object. For example, a person who has studied painting and painting tech-niques may be in a better position to appreciate the full complexity and subtly of an artwork. One may be able to see more in it—the finer details, the finesse—through having this prior training. It may also tend to heighten one's ability to enter sympathetically into the artwork if one has developed a capacity for art appreciation in the past and gained a sympathetic liking for this kind of thing. Such a person's experience of an art object will usually be richer and deeper in quality than that of the ordinary untutored person.

We might also surmise from this that the same may be the case for appreciating life and reality, or what is, or Being itself, or simply objects of awareness in general. If one has done some prior study of this matter—of philosophy, Buddhism, existentialism, physics, biology, the extraordinary depths and complexities of nature—this may have sharpened one's ability to sympathetically open to, and more deeply appreciate, the various objects of aesthetic attention, which in this case are not only art objects, but potentially all the obj-ects of awareness, all the various intricate scenes of life as they unfold. They all tend to become more marvellous and elaborate the more one probes into them and learns about them. One can never exhaust this, for there is an *infinite* amount of detail to it. Infinity—even in a grain of sand! What a shame to not be *aware* of it!

4 CONTEMPLATION

Living a contemplative life does not imply a cold or dispassionate attitude suggestive of apathetic Olympian detachment, an egocentric carelessness or an aloof disdain for mundane affairs. On the contrary, the word literally means 'the generation of a sacred space,' like a temple in which one can be engaged in the world and be re-enchanted by the everyday objects of attention—perhaps even to the point of sensing them as precious or sacred or holy, and having this feeling of warmth toward them, this interest and positive regard. One is by no means indifferent in the aesthetic attitude. One is intensely interested in all the object of awareness and in dwelling upon them aesthetically, open to their potential beauty and free delight. Given this degree of interest in the objects for their own sake alone, one can often become quite 'lost in contemplation,' as we say—rapt and fascinated by the objects of attention. At that point, contemplation may be potentiated to a maximum.

There is far less chance, at that moment, of being distracted by any other interests entering in, to impede or spoil the richness and depth of the experience. One *dwells* easily in the aesthetic state—the contemplation tends to *maintain itself*—one may even need a deliberate effort of the will to break it off and so 'come out of it'. To do this, to break the spell, one has to make a deliberate effort to do the opposite of the aesthetic; hence, re-introduce non-aesthetic elements. That is, one has to make a deliberate effort to think, to analyse, to judge, to explain, to communicate, to engage in practical activity directed toward a goal, etcetera.

Given we are by nature not only contemplative beings, but also—and much more often in our Western culture—pragmatic, intellectual and social beings, it is usually never too hard to regain this facility. In everyday life, it runs automatically, in meditative practice it tends to interrupt frequently and after deep meditation or steady contemplation it tends to rush back in with only a little solicitation.

Before finishing this brief account of the aesthetic attitude, I will mention in passing a similar account given by Kant in the first part of his book, *The Critique Of Judgment*. Like Stolnitz, Kant seems to find it easier to approach a description of what aesthetic contemplation is by way of describing what it is not. It is not a practical, utilitarian, cognitive, critical or moralistic mode of consciousness. Kant says, that in aesthetic contemplation we have, as he puts it, 'abstracted from' all the usual ways in which our minds operate in our culture. We have abstracted from the utility of the object and from the cognition of the object—labelling and thinking about it, or 'bringing it under a concept', as Kant would say. We are not concerned with that.[16]

In addition, Kant notes that we have even abstracted from the sensory agreeableness or disagreeable of the object. For we may still find an object aesthetically pleasing even if it contains some element of sensory disagreeableness.[17] For example, a discord in a musical piece might in itself be unpleasant to the ear, but it may nevertheless be aesthetically pleasing and even beautiful, when experienced in its context: the context of sympathy taken as a whole.

So, if we are focused aesthetically not merely on the objects by themselves, taking them as separated and isolated from the whole aesthetic context, but on how they stand *in relation to* the whole aesthetic background and context of *what is*, then even objects disagreeable to the senses can become beautiful: integral parts of a beautiful whole. This seems significant in light of the idea of 'letting beings be in relation to Being'. Being, or general is-ness or *what is*, is the overall context of aesthetic contemplation in which beings can stand forth and be appreciated. After all, we are not dualistically dividing and separating beings ontologically from one another or from the context of what is. Everything is simply present together, non-dualistically.

Kant also makes a distinction between what he calls 'free beauty' and what he calls 'dependent beauty'.[18] The latter refers to the beauty of perfection in design or function, when we see that a horse as beautiful insofar as it is a perfect example of the species, for example. This is called 'dependent beauty' because it depends on the application of a prior idea we have of what the object ought to be or we have a cultural standard or norm by which to assess it in relation to what it is for, its finality, its ends.

Kant seems to think more highly of dependent beauty than free beauty, probably because Kant was above all an intellectual and a moralist, rather than a pure aesthete. He tended to value and judge things in so far as they fitted in with his philosophical ideas of perfection, especially moral perfection in nature or in human beings. However, by Kant's own account of what aesthetic contemplation involves, it rather seems that 'free beauty' is the kind of beauty that best accords with it. For in dependent beauty an ideology or concept has entered in, an intellectual judgement, which is itself alien to the pure moment of aesthetic contemplation and pure aesthetic affect.

In the case of free beauty, however, no such ideology or concept enters in. For the object is not judged relative to a standard of perfection, natural or cultural. The object is appreciated simply for itself in its being, resting in itself, in abstraction from all such standards and concepts. The aesthetic experience here, then, is properly unspoilt and free, emancipated from all non-aesthetic considerations. After all, in the purest aesthetic experience, we have abstracted from even the notions of perfection of design or function, and the beauty associated with that. Free beauty is not limited to cultural beauty, since the latter is determined by accepted cultural standards. Free beauty, then, is the kind of beauty that could apply potentially to all objects of awareness. Free beauty can in principle be omni-present: everything can be beautiful in its own way, in this sense.

That will have to suffice for our brief elucidation of what is meant by a practice of the pure aesthetic attitude and the kind of free aesthetic contemplation and affect to which it may give rise in a person. Now comes an important point in Stolnitz's discussion of particular interest. For it has some implications that connect us back to our previous remarks on Heidegger, existentialism, Pyrrhonian Scepticism, and the Madhyamaka philosophy of shunyata. It will also prepare us to make a key transition from *aesthetics* to *ethics*.

EVERYTHING IS BEAUTIFUL IN ITS OWN WAY

Stolnitz says, in an initially surprising statement, that 'the aesthetic attitude can be adopted toward any object of awareness whatever,' and that, 'no object is inherently unaesthetic'.[19]

This may seem unlikely at first because, by conventional standards at any rate, only some objects are thought to be beautiful while others are thought to be aesthetically uninteresting or downright ugly. Moreover, some objects are thought to be conspicuously attractive and they strongly capture our attention, creating an aesthetic attitude in us *from without*, as it were. That is, the object itself, because of its extremely attractive qualities by some conventional cultural or personal standards, sparks off a form of the aesthetic attitude in us spontaneously, by its own power, without us having to do anything special to make ourselves sympathetically open, attentive, and receptive. The object reaches out and grabs our attention, so to speak, when hitherto we were inattentive.

It is certainly the view of commonsense and of a good deal of traditional theory of aesthetics that not all objects *are* or *can* be aesthetically pleasing. It seems some objects are inherently aesthetically pleasing or beautiful and many others displeasing or ugly. Beauty, then, will be understood as something that mainly arises from the outside in, as it were, not from the inside out; that is, not as a function of the receptive state of mind we have put ourselves in by a deliberate practice of the contemplative aesthetic attitude, but as a function of the object itself arresting our attention.

This view of the matter suggests some degree of objectivism—that beauty belongs in some sense to the object and hence to some objects rather than others—rather than it being 'in the eye of the beholder' in relation to the object: in the eye in the full sense here of being dependent on the free contemplative attitude and sympathetic receptivity of the beholder and not on the application of any criterion independent of this. Against objectivism, however, it could be pointed out that not all cultures agree on what is beautiful and ugly, so that the matter seems to be much more subjective and flexible than objectivism would suggest. Moreover, even in our own culture at different times in history different things have been seen as beautiful or ugly. For example, fashions change. Matters of taste are clearly affected to large extent by cultural and historical conditioning and so seem relative in this way. To take it further, even individuals raised in the same culture can sincerely disagree on what is beautiful or ugly. This suggests that 'the eye of the beholder' is of primary importance and that beauty exists relative to a receptive attitude.

Also, we have seen in modern times movements in art that have managed to expand the field of what can be seen to be aesthetically pleasing. For example, we have seen ordinary everyday objects being set up in art galleries. Even urinals. Because they have been placed on an art gallery wall one is encouraged to view the objects with a much more receptive and patient aesthetic attitude than one would otherwise afford them. Rather than looking at the object with a view merely to its functionality—hardly looking at it at all—one is encourage to look at it simply as an object, as a being in its own right, and so be open to its aesthetic possibilities. In this way, because we have been tricked, as it were, into being more receptive, even a urinal turned upside down may reveal some hidden beauty and become aesthetically pleasing.

In a similar vein, the avante-guard musician John Cage (1912 –1992), who was influenced by Zen, might perform a piano concerto, say, consisting of only one note and a series of rests. An audience would come in, be seated, compose themselves. The pianist would sit down at the piano and someone might stand alongside to turn the sheets of music. The pianist would play a note. Then the other person would count the rests and turn the page at the appropriate time. This could go on for perhaps half-an-hour. Meanwhile, however, there would of course be some sounds occurring in the environment; the shuffling of feet, creaking of chairs, occasional sneeze, someone walking by outside, etcetera. The point of the exercise would be to realise that all the sounds could be heard *as part of the concerto*, that is, if one listens to them all with a suitably receptive aesthetic attitude. For that pure attitude would be free from ideological prejudices and presumptions about what counts or doesn't count as music. In short, in the state of *gelassenheit*, in pure disinterest, in letting go and letting be, all sound can be experienced as music. Hence it has the potential to be felt as aesthetically pleasing.

Rather than suppose that objects of awareness are simply *given* as being either aesthetically pleasing or not, beautiful or ugly, as if this was a property in or of the objects alone and irrespective of our attitude, Stolnitz is suggesting a view that beauty exists relative to our attitude, or more precisely, it exists in the interaction between the receptive subjective attitude and the object of awareness. If so, then by cultivating an optimally receptive attitude to the objects of awareness, we may be able to greatly expand the scope of the aesthetically pleasing or beautiful; indeed, extend it potentially across all objects of awareness without preset limitation. Everything might become an aesthetic object for us and be seen as beautiful in its own way. In that case, we would not limit and restrict ourselves to only conventionally beautiful art objects or conventionally beautiful scenes of nature. Such restrictions now appear unnecessary and redundant. We do not have to depend on the pursuit and possession of special objects of beauty in order to have beauty and free delight in our lives.

When operating within conventional aesthetic boundaries, people tend to become addicted to very specific beauties—to specific people, artworks, precious things, scenes, paintings, music, events, etcetera. After all, they can only get an input of aesthetic pleasure and inspiration from those special objects, not from objects in general. Hence, they must spend considerable amounts of time and money on them, which only reinforces their addiction and personal limitations. However, if we develop in ourselves an aesthetic attitude that enables the aesthetic contemplation of free beauty, and so begin to find this free beauty and existential re-enchantment in more and more ordinary objects of awareness all around us, we could then afford to *not* be so addicted or so possessive of particular objects. We could more

easily kick that old habit. So, rather than looking to special art objects, people, or scenes of nature, etcetera, to produce in us the rich
aesthetic experience and free delight of beauty, we might do better to
look instead to cultivating the pure aesthetic attitude, an attitude to
objects that makes us optimally responsive to beauty in the whole environment of life—in 'the manifold of perception', as Kant might say.

As we have seen, this is an attitude that abstracts from utilitarian,
practical, purposive, calculative, manipulative, technical, scientific,
metaphysical, cognitive, moral and ideological considerations. We
have seen from Kant that it even abstracts from judgements regarding
perfection of design or function, and from the factor of agreeableness
or disagreeableness to the senses; hence, from the factor of sensuality
and sensory gratification (we might note in passing that aesthetic objects don't even need to be sensory ones—mathematical systems can
be regarded as elegant, symmetrical, clear, balanced and incisive and
hence, as aesthetically pleasing in nature and form).

Now, if all non-aesthetic interests are temporarily put in abeyance
and we open optimally to the object in its simple presence, letting it
stand forth as it is without interference from our side, will we not be,
in effect, meditating in the Madhyamaka Buddhist sense? For in this
meditation or contemplation we void our thinking, judging, grasping, etcetera. Here there is also something akin to the 'suspense of
judgement' that the ancient Pyrrhonian Sceptics spoke of and recommended as conducive to ataraxia and wellbeing. The practice requires
a letting go of the conceptualisations imposed on reality. We restore
ourselves to Being or to Existence Itself—to that immediate is-ness
devoided of conceptualisations. Hence, we are exercising the shunyata awareness. This seems similar also to the notion of 'letting the
rose be without why,' where we have abstracted from representational
thinking and we are letting beings be in their Being; indeed, be resplendent with Being.

There is quite a meeting here of Buddhism and existentialism.
The approach may be considered a radical kind of existentialism, because here Existence Itself precedes essence. We return to the im-

mediate upsurge of existence, here and now, in non-attachment to essentialist or metaphysical presuppositions. It may also be considered a radical kind of Buddhism, if Buddhism is understood as the shunyata philosophy, for this is also a matter of letting go of grasping at reality in concepts or grasping at special objects of desire or beauty. The way is to practise this meditative letting go of grasping; hence, it is a way of non-attachment and leads to a contemplative attitude that seems much the same, in effect, as the pure aesthetic attitude. This attitude is disinterested in the sense of being disinterested in the usual modes of consciousness; in intellectual and desire-motivated grasping. So it is also a state of *gelassenheit*. It lets things be, lets beings be in their immediacy, in which they stand forth in the context of what is as a whole.

However, we need not stipulate that in this practice there should never be any ordinary thinking going on—any language and interpretation of things. We can be aware of the diverse objects of linguistic cognition as such, but our awareness of them as being *this* or *that* is also immediately voided and annulled by insight into shunyata, into the emptiness of these cognitions. This enables non-attachment to them and to language. Therefore, we let the things of the world be as they appear for ordinary consciousness—everyday mind being the Tao—for we can, in any case, immediately void the language and the metaphysical assumptions we make as they arise in the mind. One just has to be alert and watch for it with the sword of insight. As we saw, Chogyam Trungpa Rinpoche put it this way, 'Cutting though our conceptualised version of the world with the sword of 'prajna' (insight) we discover shunyata.'[20] Or as Fredrick Streng wrote:

> The awareness of emptiness is not a blank loss of consciousness, an inanimate empty space; rather it is the cognition of daily life without the attachment to it. It is the awareness of distinct entities, of the self, of 'good' and 'bad' and other practical determinations; but it is aware of these as empty structures. Wisdom is not to be equated

with mystical ecstasy; it is rather the joy of freedom in everyday existence.[21]

In this kind of practice, we see through the metaphorical and metaphysical construction of reality *as through something that has suddenly gone transparent*. In the transparency of language, we see the unspeakable is-ness of things. *Beings become transparent in their nondual is-ness*. The sword of insight cuts straight through our conceptual systems—*suddenly, instantly*—even as we think and use them. Therefore, it is not a matter of time or of gradualness. Rather, it is as if the Veil of *Maya*, the play of illusion, the mental overlay that has covered reality, is suddenly, not *removed* as such, but *rendered transparent*. If so, then we don't have to engage in meditation exercises designed to gradually wipe away or remove or destroy or eliminate or cast aside forever the Veil of Maya. The veil doesn't have to actually *fall* to be revealing. The 'truth' of naked is-ness can be aesthetically experienced if the veil becomes transparent to our insight-awareness; for then the veil ceases to act as a veil to actually veil anything. The veil veils to no avail.

In this way, then, the everyday mind can be the Tao and one does not have to look for it anywhere else; in some special mystical or transcendental experience where the veil is supposedly lifted and eliminated altogether and absolutely, for example. It is not a matter of going 'beyond the veil' in that mystical sense and finding 'the absolute,' as if a final or ultimate state of transcending the world could be attained in this world. Rather, it is a matter of being able to instantly see through the veil of language and cognition and not be caught, fooled, enthralled, spellbound and addicted, limited by the *seeming* forms it presents; the seemingly separate things of the world, the dualism. We don't become absolutistic, we become non-dualistic.

Having said this, however, it can also be acknowledged that there can indeed be states of such intense and deep meditation that one becomes lost in contemplation—rapt in it—so absorbed that one might well lose all track of time, all sense of selfhood, all awareness of what any object is, all sense of distinctions, etcetera. We may become so completely one with the experience and with *what is* that we are not aware of *what* it is we are experiencing or even *that we are* experiencing. This is not exactly a loss of consciousness per se, but a loss of the ordinary linguistic state of spatio-temporal self-awareness of separate objects. If the mind ceases at that point to construct an experience of the world of separate beings, then there might be a sense of Oneness with the absolute. Such an experience may seem self-validating at the time. However, it is not. For if later on we attempt to communicate this experience to ourselves or to others, then we will inevitably have to use language and assert proportions, and as soon as we do then whatever we think and assert will be subject to the critical dialectic again and be consumed in sceptical suspense.

Mystics and shamans, etcetera, tend to make too much of their apparently transcendental and spiritual visions or experiences. They surely make too much of this if they think it justifies them in making dogmatic metaphysical claims—to state it as a metaphysical truth, a truth of representational thinking, that the cosmos is an organic interconnected unity, or that the self does or doesn't exist, or that everything is One or is God, or that God or the Absolute exists, etcetera. For this sort of knowledge claim would be undermined straightaway by the critical dialectic and voided. After all, any so-called 'transcendental' or 'shamanistic' experience may simply be a psychological delusion generated by the unconscious mind or by brain chemicals. Also, they make too much of it if they claim that the experience of revelation is the essential thing, is the enlightenment experience itself, and the goal we must ardently strive for in order to become enlightened beings, or Buddhas, and so reach the final ideal and find closure. For this way of thinking just spins 'the wheel of bondage' once again; it sets up a new object of desire to become attached to and at which to grasp. Consequently, people on spiritual paths to this or that future goal of so-called 'enlightenment' or 'salvation' simply generate yet more frustration and suffering. It is a path to duhkha.

It follows: there cannot be a path *to* enlightenment. There can only be a path of enlightenment. This is a path where enlightenment is cultivated by letting go of everything in the temporal world, every object of awareness, including the personal self, the past and future of the personal self, and all idealistic seeking for enlightenment or salvation for the personal self in the future. The genuine spiritual path can only be a matter of practising enlightenment timelessly in the present—hence as Ch'an in China taught: *suddenly*, not *gradually*.

Enlightenment and re-enchantment is always now: not next week, next year, next retreat, next lifetime. It is here-and-now in the midst of ordinary everyday life and within one's current situation whatever it may be. Hence it does not require travelling and going to exotic places, whether exotic places in the world or exotic places in the mind. Hence it is not a path to another place. It is a path to where one is. It is a journey without distance.

Moreover, any attempt to pursue enlightenment for the personal self as a future goal is simply more temporal egoism, more individualistic will-to-power, more self-interested seeking and grasping, hence more divisiveness and competitiveness, more 'me first,' more self-centred ambition and self-concern, more separative, alienated, and dualistic thinking. That, after all, is why Chogyam Trungpa called his book, *Cutting Through Spiritual Materialism*. Pursuing a spiritual path to something in the future, one is still acting like a materialist, in the sense of a greedy consumer, one who is now seeking to possess the new glittering item of desire, namely, spiritual enlightenment or salvation. It is quite ironic really, for usually people on a spiritual path are so critical of egocentric consumerism and materialism, and yet here they are doing fundamentally the same thing themselves: ruthlessly pursuing their own ambitions. Instead of seeking ten million dollars for oneself, one is now seeking enlightenment for oneself. There's no fundamental difference. And let's not say, 'Ah, but when I obtain the riches for myself, then I will be charitable. I will do good and help others with my riches. I'll become a great bodhisattva or saint, etcetera.' For that is often what the person seeking ten million dollars says! One says it to salve one's conscience perhaps, while the charitable part often fails to eventuate. But whether it does or doesn't, the whole procedure is a 'spiritual materialism'—the competitive will-to-power now applied to things spiritual. As such this whole divisively self-centred procedure is ethically questionable. Which brings us to our penultimate theme…

AESTHETICS AND ETHICS

It is time now to deal with a major criticism usually levelled against this kind of existentialist and aesthetic approach to life. Existentialism in general is often criticised for failing to 'provide an ethics' and for being 'beyond good and evil,' etcetera. Certainly one will be 'beyond good and evil' insofar as one has insight into the voidance of all metaphysical and moral systems. Similarly, the Madhyamaka approach and Pyrrhonism may be said to be beyond good and evil because they too criticise and reject all views, which must include all moral views. Likewise, Heidegger has frequently been criticised for failing to 'provide an ethics'.

The commonsense and conventional approach to ethics is to say, yes, people ought to be moral, so we must devise some kind of a rulebook of moral principles for the people. Then they must constantly refer to the rulebook when making their decisions and when they are tempted to deviate from the right rules they ought to engage in what Kant called 'moral combat'. That is, they ought to fight with themselves to do their duty against any inclination or temptation to deviate from this. Only in this way can the people be moral. It should be the role of the philosopher to devise such rulebooks and moral systems.

Traditionally, this is what it means to 'provide an ethics'. However, against this, the following points can be raised. The traditional approach attempts to set rules for action and then imposes these rules on people. When the rules are imposed in a particularly tyrannical and authoritarian way, and the people do not properly understand or agree with them, the chances of success are minimal, as has been shown time and time again. However, even if people understand and agree with the rules in theory, in principle, that certainly does *not* mean that they are thereby *enabled* to put them into daily practice. Rather, the result has more often been that a lot of people agree to the rules, fail to apply them as required, and then feel very *guilty* and *anxious* about it—all of which just adds yet more anguish and alienation to their already anguished and alienated lives. This just makes the whole situation worse. In this way people get caught up in a *vicious circle* of idealistic moral aspiration and failure.

Rather than devise rulebooks a more subtle and beneficial approach might be to help people transform themselves in such a way that they are enabled to act morally more easily and naturally. In other words, perhaps 'philosophical ethics' should not be about imposing rules and regulations, or essentialist moral systems, but be about recommending ways of transformation so that people can act morally every day in a more genuine and spontaneous manner—more from 'the good heart,' as the Dalai Lama often puts it. Hence, contra Kant, we would act *from* inclination, and not from duty *in opposition* to inclination. Indeed, only in this way would one act wholeheartedly, not in internal division and conflict.

Perhaps Heidegger takes a similar approach. For in his *Letter on Humanism*, when considering whether there is any connection between his meditative thinking and ethics, he says:

> If the name ethics, according to the fundamental meaning of the word 'ethos', means that it thinks the abode of man, then the thinking which thinks the Truth of Being as the primordial element of *ek-sistent* man is in itself original ethics.[22]

Let us call it 'original ethics', then, to say that we are at our most existentially authentic when we 'stand in the truth' of is-ness and shunyata. This requires a letting go of conceptual systems and therefore, a letting go of moral conceptual systems as well. Original ethics cannot be a matter of imposing rational or religious moral systems, duties and rules of action, but rather of letting them go. However, this *amorality* does not result in *immorality*. Rather, it is through the authentic experience of being with things in the mode of meditation and aesthetic contemplation that we are gradually transformed. We become more sensitive to the aesthetic quality, value, awe, beauty, glory, meaning and wonderment of what is, just so, as we live and breathe in each moment without why.

This kind of aesthetic attitude and aesthetic experience of life begins to have a healing effect on our affections, our passions. We are no longer so interested in the old manipulative and strategic ways of thinking and acting. Nor are we so interested in the egocentric will-to-power as it tries to competitively grasp after things for oneself intellectually and passionately—even on so-called spiritual paths. Our increasing appreciation of what is, and our here-and-now sense of affinity with what is, makes us feel less alienated in life, hence more grounded. We feel centred in life rather than in the ego. Accordingly, we tend to feel more benevolent and sympathetically disposed in general: toward the environment, toward nature, and toward all the beings in their is-ness that we encounter along the way. Of course this extends to people too, and to ourselves, everything included. With this new more holistic and aesthetically receptive way of living and acting we acquire a greater capacity to be moral naturally from the heart. It tends to follow we will be less inclined to lie, cheat, kill, steal, break promises, be fickle, angry, violent, over-anxious, ruthless, or act with greed or hostility, etcetera.

We are now approaching something akin to that saying usually ascribed to St. Augustine (350–430 AD), 'Love, and do what thou wilt!'

If we have a wellspring of sympathy, affinity, and love within us due to our way of being in the non-dual aesthetic appreciation of what is, being more at one and in tune with it in peace and harmony, it is likely that 'virtue' will come more easily and naturally as a matter of transformed inclination. We will not be in need of moral rule-books. Moreover, it will be easier for us to be moral in good spirits;

that is, in *eudemonia*. The action will emerge and express itself more cheerfully and spontaneously, like ripe fruit dropping from the vine. *Arête* (virtue, excellence in action) is naturally associated with eudemonia (having a good spirit within) in this way.

Also, we will not be so divisive or half-hearted in our actions. For one of the problems with the conventional approach to morality is that, even when people do manage to act morally according to the rules, they usually do so rather begrudgingly, feeling they are making a sacrifice, also feeling rather self-righteous about it and consequently, feeling that they are owed some sort of reward, recognition, or even praise. Indeed, they can get quite annoyed about it if they feel they are not getting the recognition they believe they deserve for their obedience to the rules. However, if people act morally from a source of inner wellbeing, as a kind of *overflowing* in abundance from that source, they will tend to act in good spirits and not feel that their action is a big sacrifice, that they need, that they ought to get some additional reward for it, some entitlement. They will feel the action is its own reward. Who needs recognition? Who's keeping a tally?

THE AESTHETICS OF LOVE

Is it reasonable to assume that this meditative entering into the experience of the non-dual aesthetic quality of Existence Itself, or Being, or Nothingness, is likely to be conducive to an emotional transformation in the general direction of a free and holistic love?

It seems plausible for the following reason. What begets in us a spontaneous feeling of love for something, whether it is love for an art object, for nature, for persons? Rather obviously, it seems, we naturally tend to feel *love* toward something we find *lovable*. And, it seems, what makes something more lovable to us is that we see and appreciate its beauty. *We tend to love that which we find beautiful*. As Kant says, 'The beautiful prepares us to love something, even nature, apart from any interest.'[23]

There is this kind of connection between aesthetic appreciation and the loving response. Now, unfortunately, for most of us most of the time, we are very limited and narrow in what we can love. That is no doubt because we are very limited and narrow in what we can find beautiful. We feel limited to this or that particular person, or a few people, or just these or those special objects. Our love is very specific. And because it is very specific we easily become habitually attached, even seriously addicted, to those very specific objects—possessions, persons, family, nation, church, etcetera. We have to have just those ones because they are the only ones we can love. Romantic and family loves are clear examples of this; forms of love that are limited in scope to a very few people, or even just one. This seems almost as petty and narrow as just loving oneself. Indeed, it is sometimes said that a romantic-sexual love relationship is 'an egoism of two'. As such, these common forms of love seem greatly overrated in modern/postmodern culture today, especially in the mass media.

Is there a way we can expand the whole scope of love? It's an interesting and highly practical question, one with many implications for morality. Well, as we have said, if love tends to be a natural response to the beautiful as such, and we have found we can expand the scope of the beautiful, then it should be possible to expand the scope of love accordingly. We can now add, that there is not one, but two ways of doing this.

First, we might expand the scope of the beautiful by practising the pure aesthetic attitude of non-dual contemplation toward everything and so let beings be without why, voided in their is-ness. If we can make the ultimate object of aesthetic appreciation this strange factor of non-dual is-ness, this strange attractor that reveals itself in the objects of awareness in the voided and contemplative attitude, and if we can wait receptively to let ourselves be positively affected by it, then perhaps this source of spontaneous free beauty, this free delight, and this free affection for all, will be potentially available to us everywhere. If we can tune into that beauty of non-dual is-ness, the experience can be a source of a subtle inspiration that modifies the feelings and passions in the general direction of increasing *ataraxia*

and *metriopatheia*—greater serenity, inner wellbeing, peace of mind, and a natural temperance in regard to preferences and actions in the world. We are not much troubled and bothered by our projects and goals because, in the virtue of temperance, one is not driven or controlled by desires. Rather, one is non-attached. Therefore, our engagement in action in the world is also disengagement; i.e., our action is a mode of play. In short, we have playful preferences or temperate preferences, meaning preference that we can take or leave.

2)   Second, inspired in this way by the aesthetic experience of non-dual is-ness, and taking temperate action in the world motivated by a playful creative preference, free existential subjectivity can reconstitute and reaffirm the totality of life as good and beautiful through and through by positing it poetically as the theatrical play of the one transpersonal Joyful Player. So, as already a player acting with a playful preference, we posit the Joyful Player as the one divine Self in each one of us, the world as its divine theatre for diversity of experiences and temporal dramas, and all sentient egos everywhere as its multiple personas. Persons are the personas in time of the one transpersonal timeless Player, while what we really are behind the mask of temporal selfhood, in our innermost self, is the pure I in itself —the Playmaker, the one timeless Self that creates the set of experiences we call life in the world. And in short, on this view it seems that Shakespeare was right all along in saying, 'All the world's a stage and we are the players.'[24] The world is the Globe Theatre, the world theatre as it were, the Rose Theatre—and the rose is without why. But now we also perceive that each petal of the rose, and every one of its thorns too, is an interconnected or interdependent beauty in the one beautiful whole.

Hence: we have both free beauty and interdependent beauty in this double game.

As our poetic preference here is played out in the virtue of temperance, we can take it or leave it. Accordingly, this painting of things transcendental and metaphysical—or perhaps we should take a lead from Jean Baudrillard (1929–2007) and call it 'pataphysical,' a 'science of imaginary solutions,' that is post-the-postmodern.[25] It is not a religious or a rationalist dogma, not an objective truth, not even a (Kierkegaard-like) subjective truth, or any other kind of representational truth. For it is not a truth at all. It no longer pretends to be a truth representing reality, because it is post-metaphysical, post-representational, post-theoretical, post-critical, and post-deconstructive. For these reasons, it is even post-postmodern. Truth is dead. Ideology is dead. Deconstruction is dead, Modernism/postmodernism is dead. For it is time now to leave the nineteenth and twentieth centuries behind and move on. Move on to what? Well, Heidegger and Baudrillard suggest a way: toward poetic thinking, pataphysical thinking, re-enchantment thinking, a thinking that is rooted first in voidance, that operates from there and returns home to there.

As the pataphysical is not a truth, we are pleased to be able to take it or leave it—for, of course, we like it that we are unattached. That is our ludic temperance with regards to this piece of pataphysical poetry. Nevertheless, we are also pleased to posit it in goodwill, as inspired by the holistic good feeling about life that spontaneously arises from the void aesthetic contemplation of non-dual isness. Goodwill prompts us to pronounce it, as our preferred theatre of imaginary solutions, that we are 'all perfect altogether,' as Max Stirner said—or that we are the one immortal and timeless God, that we are all divine, that we are the one Player in the one Play. Hence there is no evil in creation, and no evil person to be found anywhere. There are no separations, no exclusions. Not only is 'the innocence of becoming' restored to us in all its glory (as Nietzsche might wish)[26] but more—the whole is made positively good, and the real ideal (as Stirner might wish).[27] Thus everything can be appropriated by free subjectivity for comprehensive self-enjoyment.

Not only that, but this way of painting things lets us regard the totality of life with 'unconditional positive regard,' to borrow a handy phrase from the psychotherapist, Carl C. Rogers (1902—1987).[28] Then this unconditional positive regard better enables us to open ourselves to what is with precisely that 'sympathetic receptivity' required by the aesthetic attitude. Thus, *the positive pataphysical picture better enables the aesthetic contemplation of non-dual is-ness that inspires the goodwill that posits the positive pataphysical picture.*

Yes, in short, what we have here is the opposite of a vicious circle—which I suppose might be called a virtuous circle. One side feeds the other side of this double game and the two sides go spiralling on in increasing charm and re-enchantment. In love, we *elect* to take the most *charitable* view of reality, that it is all good, all one, all divine. And as a result we are enabled to be more receptive to whatever is in aesthetic contemplation. Beauty inspires love, love inspires beauty. As the opposite of the wheel of bondage, there is this wheel of freedom.

If we make the totality of existence our first love, the ultimate object of love, our love will not then be small, petty, narrow and limited to just a few people or particular things. Rather it will be a comprehensive love. This does not mean that we cannot have our limited particular loves too: sexual loves, or family loves or friendship loves, etcetera. It means that these limited particular loves become secondary to the holistic love, the love of totality, the comprehensive love. And that means that our particular loves will no longer be a source of 'trouble' in life, or duhkha. How so? Because if or when we lose this or that particular object of love—someone dies, a lover walks out, a friend is lost in the passage of time, our house burns down—we are able to let it go in the general movement of life without attachment.

Note: we are not unattached here because we are lacking in love—as some folk may think, if they do not understand this philosophy correctly—but because we are full of love, namely, holistic love. For where there is comprehensive love, then there is no attachment. In other words, attachment is associated with incomplete and immature love, while non-attachment is associated with comprehensive and mature love. Our culture is so muddle-headed about this—no doubt we watch too many Hollywood movies and it is rotting our brains!—it is actually widely believed that love and attachment go together. In fact, the opposite is the case: attachment arises when there is *not enough* love. Moreover, the recipe for a broken heart, is not to love less, but to love more. That is, love more comprehensively, less narrowly. Contrary to what is usually said about love, let's try this instead:

> Love is never a matter of a particular obsession, infatuation or idolatry; it is not manipulation, domination control, or direction; is it not possessiveness, jealousy, anxiety or insecurity; it is not about duty, vows, guilt, monogamy or exclusivity; nor is it fickleness, inconstancy, promiscuity or greed; and it is not emotional need, attachment, addiction or co-dependency. Love will not enslave us, love will set us free. Love is freedom and love promotes freedom. Only free spirits can love.

Remember though, that it is not a matter of seeking this love in time. We do not come to this love in time; we come to love in the timeless now. For love is holistic, and to be holistic it must love everything, and if it loves everything then it loves what already has been and is—now. This is perfectly logical. On the other hand, if one seeks love elsewhere, in a different place, in the future, in a drug, in a special experience, in a church, in a retreat, in the next world, etcetera, one is merely reinforcing the dualism, the particularism, the exclusivity, and that is contrary to love when love is understood comprehensively. *One moves away from love in the very act of trying to move toward it.* No wonder people find their so-called spiritual paths so frustrating! This too is tanha and duhkha. In fact, a spiritual path to love is a contradiction in terms.

However, there can be a path of love, a path where each present moment is the centre and fount of love, just as it is, just where you always are, now. And this love spreads out from there in an overflow to all and everything, to one-in-all and all-in-one without division, without divisiveness—to the one Buddha-mind or Buddha-self that is everything and everyone as one interconnected whole. It is the path of *gelassenheit*.

In sum: The path of love is the practice of letting everything go in comprehensive voidance and non-attachment and letting everything be in comprehensive unity and charity. One moves from emptiness to fullness and back again.

Gelassenheit enables love. Gelassenheit is original ethics, fundamental morality. To provide an ethics is to provide a philosophy of gelassenheit.

Love is virtue, it is arête/eudemonia. Together they constitute wisdom—*sophia*. Philosophy is the love of wisdom. Therefore, properly understood, philosophy is the practice of gelassenheit, philosophy is the love of love.

Finally, life is whole, undivided, wholesome and ideal; indeed, it is holy (from Old English, *halig*, meaning 'hale, healthy, whole, wholesome'). Every present moment is like a new beginning, a fresh start, the first and last moment, and our mind is always 'a beginner's mind' as Zen Master Shunryu Suzuki Roshi (1904–1971) says.[29] He also said, 'From true emptiness, wondrous being.'[30] In other words, from the void of this moment, we begin again in holistic love. Then each moment is a good moment to die and a good moment to live. This will be, as Krishnamurti put it, 'the first and last freedom'.[31]

In Letting Go and Letting Be
One is the Beauty of the Rose Without Why.

NOTES

CHAPTER ONE

[1] Ludwig Wittgenstein, *Tractatus Logico-Philosophicus*, Routledge, 2001, section 7.

[2] See Alan Watts, *The Way of Zen*, Penguin Arkana, 1990, p. 112.

[3] See Frederick J. Streng, *Emptiness: A Study in Religious Meaning*, Abingdon Press, 1967, p. 76.

[4] Ibid., p. 76 and *passim*.

[5] Ibid., p. 159.

[6] See Ayya Khema's *Being Nobody, Going Nowhere*, Wisdom Publications, 1987.

[7] Watts, Ibid., p. 112.

[8] The tirle of Alan Keightley's, *Into Every Life A Little Zen Must Fall*, Wisdom Publications, 1987.

[9] Watts, ibid., chapter four, *passim*.

[10] Hu Shih, 'Ch'an (Zen) Buddhism in China: Its History and Method,' in the journal, *Philosophy East and West*, 1953, Vol. 3, p. 3.

CHAPTER TWO

[1] See Friedrich Nietzsche, *Beyond Good and Evil*, Penguin Classics, Part 1, Section 3.

[2] Rene Descartes, *A Discourse on Method and Meditations*, Everyman's Library, 1969, meditation three, p. 96.

[3] See Hilary Putnam, *Reason, Truth and History*, Cambridge, University Press, 1981, pp. 5–8.

[4] Nietzsche, ibid. book one, section 16.

[5] Bertrand Russell, *The Analysis of Mind*, Cosimo Classics, 2004, pp.

159–60.

[6] See Philip P. Hallie (ed.), *Sextus Empiricus: selections from the major writings*, Avatar Books, 1985, pp. 9 & 79.

[7] David Hume, A Treatise on Human Nature, Penguin Classics, 1969, Part IV, Section 1, Of Scepticism with Regard to Reason, p. 237.

[8] Hallie, ibid., p. 7, 35n & p. 14, 42n.

[9] Hallie, ibid., p. 13, 42n.

[10] Benson Mates, trans. *The Skeptic Way: Sextus Empiricus's Outlines of Pyrrhonism*, Oxford University Press, 1996, pp. 92–93.

[11] Ibid., p. 93.

[12] Ibid., p. 93.

CHAPTER THREE

[1] Jean-Paul Sartre, 'Existentialism Is A Humanism,' reprinted in Walter Kaufmann (ed.), *Existentialism From Dostoevsky To Sartre*, 1975, p. 348.

[2] Soren Kierkegaard, *The Journals Of Kierkegaard*, translated by Alexander Dru, Fontana 3 Books, 1958, pp. 90–1.

[3] Ibid., p. 44.

[4] Ibid., p. 98.

[5] Ibid., p. 89.

[6] Max Stirner, *The Ego and His Own*, trans. Steven T. Byington, Dover Edition, 2005, p. 86.

[7] Ibid., p. 366.

[8] Ibid., p. 14.

[9] Ibid., p. 67.

[10] Ibid., p. 139.

[11] Ibid., p. 315.

[12] Ibid., p. 185.

[13] Ibid., p. 366.

[14] For comment on this see John D. Caputo, *The Mystical Element in Heidegger's Thought*, Ohio Uni. Press, 1990, pp. 247–249.

[15] Sartre, ibid., p. 353.

[16] Stirner, ibid, p. 315.

[17] Ibid., pp. 319–321.

[18] Sartre ibid., pp. 367–8.

[19] Stirner, ibid., p. 362.

[20] Ibid., p. 359.

[21] Sartre ibid., p. 353.

[22] Edward Conze, *Buddhism: It's Evolution and Development*, Cassirer Publishers, Oxford, 1960, pp. 22–23.

[23] Frederick J. Streng, *Emptiness: A Study In Religious Meaning*, Abingdon Press, 1975, pp. 159–160.

[24] Chogyam Trungpa, *Cutting Through Spiritual Materialism*, Shambhala Publications, 1973, p. 187.

[25] *Hamlet*, Act 2, Scene 2, p. 249.

[26] See, for example, David D. Burns, *Feeling Good: The New Mood Therapy*, Avon, 1999.

[27] See Alan Watts, *The Way Of Zen*, Penguin Arkana, 1957, Part 2, Chapter 2.

CHAPTER FOUR

[1] For an excellent discussion of this topic see R. G. Olsen, *An Introduction To Existentialism*, Dover, 1962, pp. 197–201.

[2] See John D. Caputo, *The Mystical Element In Heidegger's Thought*, Ohio University Press, 1990, p. 24.

[3] Ibid., p. 58.

[4] Ibid., p. 4.

[5] Ibid., pP. 21–22.

[6] Ibid., p. 29.

[7] Ibid., p. 80.

[8] Ibid., pP. 1–6.

[9] See Martin Heidegger, *The End Of Philosophy*, trans. J. Stambaugh, University Of Chicago Press, 2003.

[10] Caputo, ibid., p. 27.

[11] Ibid., p. 247.

[12] Ibid., p. 78.

[13] Ibid., p. 191–2.

[14] Ibid., pp. 247–9.

[15] Martin Heidegger, *The Principle Of Reason*, trans. Reginald Lilly, Indiana University Press, 1991.

[16] For an extended discussion of this, see Caputo, ibid, Chapter 2, pp. 47–96.

[17] Ibid., pg 53.

[18] See Caputo, ibid., pp. 9, 40 & 61.

[19] Ibid., pp. 9, 40 & 61ff.

[20] Ibid., pp. 4 & 6.

[21] Ibid., pp. 118–9.

[22] Ibid., p. 88.

[23] Ibid., p. 248.

[24] Ibid., p. 247.

[25] Stirner, ibid, p. 296.

[26] From the music album Wee Tam & The Big Huge, the song 'Maya,' by the *The Incredible String Band*, Electra, 1968.

CHAPTER FIVE

[1] Immanuel Kant, *The Critique of Judgement*, trans. James Creed Meredith, Oxford University Press,1980, First Part, First Book, pp. 41–90.

[2] Edward Bullough, *Aesthetics*, Stanford University Press, 1977.

[3] Jerome Stolnitz, *Aesthetics and the Philosophy of Art Criticism*, Houghton Mifflin Co., 1960.

[4] John Hospers, *Introductory Readings In Aesthetics*, Collier Macmillan, 1969.

[5] Carolyn Korsmeyer, *Aesthetics: The Big Questions*, Blackwell, 1998.

[6] Kant, ibid., p. 49.

[7] Stolnitz, all quotations taken from the Korsmeyer reprint, p. 78.

[8] Richard Gregory, *The Eye and Brain*, Princeton University Press, 5th Edition, 1997.

[9] Stolnitz, ibid., p. 78.

[10] See David D. Burns, *Feeling Good: The New Mood Therapy*, Avon Books, 1999.

[11] Stolnitz, ibid., p. 80.

[12] See Raymond B. Blakney, *Meister Eckhart: a modern translation*, Harper & Row, 1941, p. 41 and Matthew Fox, *Breakthrough: Meister Eckhart's Creation Spirituality in a New Translation*, Doubleday Books, 1980.

[13] Ibid., p. 80.

[14] Ibid., p. 81.

[15] *The Cloud of Unknowing*, ed. William Johnston, Image Books, 1996.

[16] Kant, ibid., p. 42.

[17] Ibid., p. 44.

[18] Ibid., p. 72.

[19] Stolnitz, ibid., p. 83.

[20] Chogyam Trungpa, *Cutting Through Spiritual Materialism*, Shambhala Publications, 1973, p. 187.

[21] Frederick J. Streng, *Emptiness: A Study in Religious Meaning*, Abingdon Press, 1975, pp. 159–60.

[22] Cited in Caputo, ibid., pp. 255–6.

[23] Kant ibid., p. 119.

[24] Shakespeare, *As You Like It*, Act 2, 7:139.

[25] Jean Baudrillard, *Fatal Strategies*, trans. P. Beitchman & W. G. J. Niesluchowski, Semiotext(e)/Plato Publications, 1990, p. 85.

[26] Friedrich Nietzsche, *Twilight Of The Idols, The Antichrist*, trans. R. J. Holingdale, Penguin Classics, 1968, p. 54.

[27] Max Stirner, ibid., p. 362.

[28] See Carl R. Rogers, *Client Centred Therapy*, Trans-Atlantic Pubs, 1995.

[29] From the title *Zen Mind, Beginner's Mind*, by Shunryu Suzuki Roshi, Weatherhill, 1970, p. 105.

[30] Ibid., p. 105.

[31] The title of Jiddu Krishnamurti's, *The First and Last Freedom*, Gollancz, 1972.

BIBLIOGRAPHY

Abe, Masao. *Zen and Western Thought*, University Of Hawai'i Press, 1989.

Ayya Khema, *Being Nobody, Going Nowhere*, Wisdom, Publications, 1987.

Batchelor, Stephen. *Buddhism Without Beliefs: A Contemporary Guide to Awakening*, Riverhead Books, 1997.

——. *Faith To Doubt: Glimpses of Buddhist Uncertainty*, Parallax Press, 1990.

Baudrillard, Jean. *Fatal Strategies,* translated by P. Beitchman & W. G. J. Niesluchowski, Semiotext(e)/Plato Pubs., 1990.

Blakney, Raymond B. trans and intro. *Meister Eckhart: a modern translation*, Harper & Row, 1941.

Bullough, Edward. *Aesthetics*, Stanford University Press, 1977.

Burns, David. *Feeling Good: The New Mood Therapy*, Avon, 1999.

Caputo, John D. *The Mystical Element in Heidegger's Thought*, Ohio University Press, 1990.

Conze, Edward. *Buddhism: Its Evolution and Development*, Cassirer Publishers, Oxford, 1960.

Descartes, Rene. *A Discourse On Method And Meditations On First Philosophy,* Everyman Library, 1969.

Eckhart, Meister. *Breakthrough: Meister Eckhart's Creation Spirituality in a New Translation*, Doubleday Books, 1980.

——. *Meditations with Meister Eckhart*, ed. Matthew Fox, Bear & Co., 1983.

Fromm, Erich. *To Have or To Be?* Abacus Books, 1979.

Garfield, Jay L. *Empty Words: Buddhist Philosophy and Cross-cultural Interpretation*, Oxford University Press, 2001.

Gregory, Richard L. *Eye and Brain*, Princeton University Press, 1997.

Hadot, Pierre. *Philosophy as a Way of Life: Spiritual Exercises from Socrates to Foucault*, Blackwell Publishers, 1995.

——. *What is Ancient Philosophy?* trans. by M. Chase, Belknap Press, 2004.

Heidegger, Martin. *The Principle of Reason*, trans. by Reginald Lilly, Indiana University Press, 1996.

——. *The Question Concerning Technology and Other Essays*, trans. by William Lovitt, Harper & Row, 1977.

Holroyd, Stuart. *Krishnamurti: The Man, The Mystery, The Message*, Element Books, 1991.

Hospers, John. *Introductory Readings in Aesthetics*, Collier-Macmillan, 1969.

Hume, David. *A Treatise on Human Nature*, Penguin Classics, 1969.

Huntington, C. W. *The Emptiness of Emptiness: An Introduction to Early Indian Madhyamika*, University of Hawai'i Press, 1989.

Hu Shih. 'Ch'an Buddhism in China: Its History and Method,' in *Philosophy East and West*, University of Hawai'i Press, April, 1953.

Kant, Immanuel. *The Critique of Judgement*, trans. by James Creed Meredith, Oxford University Press, 1980.

Kaufmann, Walter A. *Existentialism from Dostoevsky to Sartre*, Meridian Books, 1975.

Keightley, Alan. *Into Every Life a Little Zen Must Fall*, Wisdom Publications, 1987.

Kierkegaard, Soren. Robert Bretall, (ed.) *A Kierkegaard Anthology*, Princeton University Press, 1951.

——. *Concluding Unscientific Postscript*, trans. D. F. Swenson & W. Lowrie, Princeton University Press, 1968.

——. *The Journals Of Kierkegaard*, trans. Alexander Dru, Fontana Books, 1958.

Korsmeyer, Carolyn. *Aesthetics: The Big Questions*, Blackwell, 1998.

Krishnamurti, Jiddu. *Freedom From The Known*, Krishnamurti Foundation India, 2004.

——. *The Awakening of Intelligence*, Harper One, 1987.

——. *The First And Last Freedom*, Gollancz, 1972.

Marino, Gordon. (ed.). *Basic Writings of Existentialism*, Modern Library Classics, 2004.

Mates, Benson. *The Sceptic Way: Sextus Empiricus's Outlines of Pyrrhonism*, Oxford University Press, 1996.

May, Reinhard. *Heidegger's Hidden Sources: East-Asian Influences on His Work*, Routledge, 1996.

Murti, T. R. V. *The Central Philosophy of Buddhism*, Munshirm Manoharlal Publishers, 2003.

Nagarjuna. *The Fundamental Wisdom of the Middle Way: Nagarjuna's Mulamadhyamakarika*, trans. by Jay L. Garfield, Oxford University Press, 1995.

Nietzsche, Friedrich. *Beyond Good and Evil*, trans. by R. J. Hollingdale, Penguin Classics, 1973.

———. *The Twilight of the Idols* and *The Antichrist*, trans. by R. J. Hollingdale, Penguin Classics, 1968.

Olsen, Robert G. *An Introduction to Existentialism*, Dover, 1962.

Pirsig, Robert M. *Zen and the Art of Motorcycle Maintenance*, Harper Torch, 2006.

Plato, *Apology*, trans. by James J. Helm, Bolchazy-Carducci Publishers, 1997.

Popkin, Richard, H. *The History of Scepticism from Erasmus to Spinoza*, University of California Press, 1979.

Rupp, George. *Beyond Existentialism and Zen*, Oxford University Press, 1979.

Sartre, Jean Paul. *Existentialism is a Humanism*, trans. by Carol Macomber, Yale University Press, 2007.

Seung Sahn. *Only Don't Know: The Teaching Letters of Zen Master Seung Sahn*, Primary Point Press, 1982.

Sextus Empiricus, edited by Philip P. Hallie, *Sextus Empiricus: Selection from the Major Writings on Scepticism, Man and God*, Avatar Books, 1985.

———. *Outlines of Pyrrhonism*, Great Books in Philosophy, trans. by R .G. Bury, Prometheus Books, 1990.

———. *Outlines of Scepticism*, (Cambridge Texts in the History of Philosophy), edited by Julia Annas, Cambridge University Press, 2000.

Shunru Suzuki Roshi, *Zen Mind, Beginner's Mind*, Weatherhill, 1970.

Silesius, Angelus and Frederick Franck, *The Book of Angelus Silesius*, Random House, 1976.

Stirner, Max. *The Ego and His Own*, trans. by Steven T. Byington, Dover
   Publishers, 2005.

Stolnitz, Jerome. *Aesthetics and the Philosophy of Art Criticism*, Houghton
   Mifflin, 1960.

Streng, Frederick J. *Emptiness: A Study in Religious Meaning*, Abingdon Press,
   1975.

Suzuki, D. T. *Mysticism: Christian and Buddhist*, Dover, 2002.

Tolle, Eckhart. *Stillness Speaks*, New World Library, 2003.

———. *The Power of Now*, New World Library, 2004.

Trungpa, Chogyam. *Cutting Through Spiritual Materialism*, Shambhala
   Publications, 1973.

Watts, Alan W. *The Way of Zen*, Pantheon Books, 1999.

Wittgenstein, Ludwig. *Tractatus Logico-Philosophicus*, Routledge, 2001.

INDEX

Christianity, 64, 86
clearness, 95–99, 124
clearing, 9, 90–92, 99
closed circle, 38–39, 111
cloud of forgetting, 124
cogito ergo sum, 43
commitments, 52, 78, 123
    fallible, 22, 40, 78–79,
    82–83, 113
concepts, 2–4, 59, 68
    grasping, 27, 30, 91, 133
    voided, 9, 25
conceptual constructions, 3–13,
16, 20–21, 68–69
conceptual systems, 69, 83, 89,
    91, 134, 138
conformity, 62, 64
consciousness, 67–68, 124, 133
    false, 90–94
consumerism, 89, 112, 136
contemplation, 84–85
    aesthetic, 85, 113–14, 126–34
    moment of, 21, 54, 113
    shunyata-, 25
    voided, 114, 121–23, 143–44
Conze, Edward, 80
cosmological argument, 101–2
craving, 2, 14
creation scientists, 38
critical dialectic, 4–5, 12–16, 20,
    49, 52, 135
critical insight, 9, 12–13
cultural conditioning, 23, 130
cure, 4, 12, 20, 112

D

Dalia Lama, 138
death, 15, 52, 56, 72–74
    live toward, 87
deception, 40–42, 45, 47
decisions, 21–22
de-concenptualising, 12
deconstruction, 21, 92, 143
Delphic oracle, 46
demonic, 23, 39
Descartes, Rene, 40, 42–44
de-reflection, 114
Derrida, 47
desire, 19
    objects of, 14–15, 27, 54–55,
    133–36
detachment, 5, 126
determinism, 43
deviod, 6, 9, 52, 121
discipline, 17, 19, 26
disease, 2, 14, 16, 20
disengagement, 142
    engaged, 79, 83, 111, 114
disinterest, 119, 121, 131
dispassionate, 121, 126
disquiet, 7, 12
dissolve, 6–7, 67–68
distraction, 124
divine, 113
    artisan, 60
    player, 114–15, 143–44
divinity, 109
divisiveness, 70, 136, 145
doubt, 43–45, 72

first and last, 146
futility, 50, 108

G

gelassenheit, 109, 114, 119, 124,
131, 133, 145–46
Ginsberg, Allen, 1, 5
God, 17, 23, 34–35, 37–38,
40–41, 60, 75, 77, 90, 103,
109–11, 135, 143
as first cause, 97, 100–2, 110
deceptive, 47
is dead, 88
Gollum, 109
goodness, 41, 54, 84, 113
goodwill, 143–44
gospels, 6, 37, 96
Grand Unified Theory, 100
grasping, 6, 8, 11–14, 108, 133
Gregory, Richard, 117
ground, 8–10, 15, 68, 90–91,
95, 99, 103, 106–8
groundless-, 91, 106–7
groundlessness, 102

H

habits, 118, 123
halig, 146
hallucination, 35
hang-ups, 5–7, 10, 14, 28
happiness, 2–3, 16–18, 62, 92
harmony, 3, 15, 70, 84, 113
heart, 27, 64, 122, 138–39, 144
Hegel, Georg Wilhelm, 63–65

Heidegger, Martin, 68, 74,
86–90, 92–111, 118, 128,
137–38, 143
holistic, 84–85, 114–15, 139
affirmation, 76, 83, 113
love, 140, 144–46
Hospers, John, 116
hostile, 15, 70, 112
Hu Shih, 27
Hui-Neng, 26
Hume, David, 50
humorous, 25

I

ideals, 15–16, 19, 62
ideology, 77, 123, 128, 143
ignoble, 16
illusion, 25, 47, 56, 71, 134
comforting, 74, 80
imaginary, 5, 7–8, 13, 142–43
immediacy, 21, 25, 108, 133
immediate existence, 8, 44,
61–62, 68
immediate presence, 97, 122
immorality, 139
impermanence, 2
inauthentic, 80, 89
inclination, 137–39
infinite regress, 101, 104–5
infinity, 25
ignoble, 16
insight, 11, 17–18, 26, 28, 108,
133–34, 137
critical, 9, 12–13